building small

sustainable designs for tiny houses & backyard buildings

david & jeanie stiles

illustrations by david stiles

POPULAR WOODWORKING BOOKS

CINCINNATI, OHIO

popularwoodworking.com

building small

sustainable designs
for tiny houses &
backyard buildings

david & jeanie stiles

illustrations by david stiles

DEDICATION
To William Stiles Catlett, already showing great promise with a hammer.

ACKNOWLEDGMENTS
We would like to thank our editor, Scott Francis, for his enthusiasm and support throughout the writing and production of this book. Both he and art director Daniel Pessell respected our vision and never lost sight of it.

Thanks also to Toby Haynes for his copy- and photo-editing, attention to detail and ability to keep a cool head during moments of chaos; to Simon Jutras for his time and skill shooting beautiful photographs; and of course to the many small house builders who shared their visions, experiences and photos so generously.

about the authors

DAVID AND JEANIE STILES have written a total of 25 "how-to" books on building projects: from treehouses and forts, to sheds, gazebos and garden houses, and have sold over one-million copies. Their two most recent books are "Treehouses and Playhouses You Can Build" and "Backyard Buildings." They have received several awards, including the ALA's Notable Children's Book Award for "Treehouses You Can Actually Build." Their work has appeared in *Architectural Digest*, *House Beautiful*, *Better Homes and Gardens*, *Country Living* and *The New York Times*. Television appearances include HGTV and the Discovery Channel; on "The Today Show" they even built a treehouse during a single live three-hour broadcast from Rockefeller Center.

David and Jeanie divide their time between New York City and East Hampton, N.Y. where they live in a barn they renovated themselves; here they build many of the projects featured in their books.

contents

introduction

The Tiny House movement started in the late 1960s and 70s, when the hip generation began building their own houses in the woods or wherever they could buy land cheap. Writers such as Lloyd Kahn (*Shelter Magazine*), Lester Walker ("The Tiny House Book"), Stewart Brand (The Whole Earth Catalog) and Ken Kern ("The Owner Built Home") recognized that these inexperienced carpenters needed Do-It-Yourself guides. The results were often innovative – for example the use of ferro-cement, inflatable structures, Buckminster Fuller's geodesic domes and straw-bale construction. The rise of solar and geothermal technologies enabled people to live off the grid.

More recently, the idea of the owner-built house has been overtaken by new concerns over global warming and our carbon footprint: *eco-friendly* and *sustainable* are now mainstream terms. For various reasons, many people are downsizing their homes, workspaces, leisure spaces and possessions. Downsizing does not only apply to houses but has become a mindset and way of life.

People often think a tiny house is a trailer on wheels, but this is not necessarily so – it can be on solid foundations or even a floating houseboat. (In our book "Rustic Retreats," we describe a tiny 7' x 7' recreational cabin built on foam billets and transported to and from the water by car.) Tiny houses on wheels are easy to transport, but we think this places excessive restrictions on the dimensions (in order to meet highway requirements). If necessary, a tiny house without its own wheels – such as our Tudor backyard building – can be moved on a flatbed truck or trailer.

OUR STORY

We always dreamed of a weekend retreat no more than fifty miles from our New York City apartment. One day, we set off in our Mini Moke jeep (rather than making an appointment with a broker) and headed north to see what was available within an hour of the city. We checked the papers for acreage for sale – today, of course, the Internet would be a useful resource. As luck would have it, our car overheated and we serendipitously met a local woman raking leaves. She had bought and built on land nearby, and gave us the name of her source – a terrific woman who was selling off parcels of her estate. It's amazing what you can discover by driving around an area and getting to know the people who live there. We were able to buy 25 acres of land very reasonably. We used it as a source of pleasure – hiking and picnicking on it – while we imagined and sketched ideas for our weekend house. There's nothing like camping out on a piece of property to discover where the sun rises and falls. We spent many happy hours designing our futuristic dream house before we suddenly realized all we needed was a cabin. We didn't want the expense, hassle and responsibility of a full-size dwelling. We wanted a tiny house to escape from the city, to enjoy nature and a simpler life.

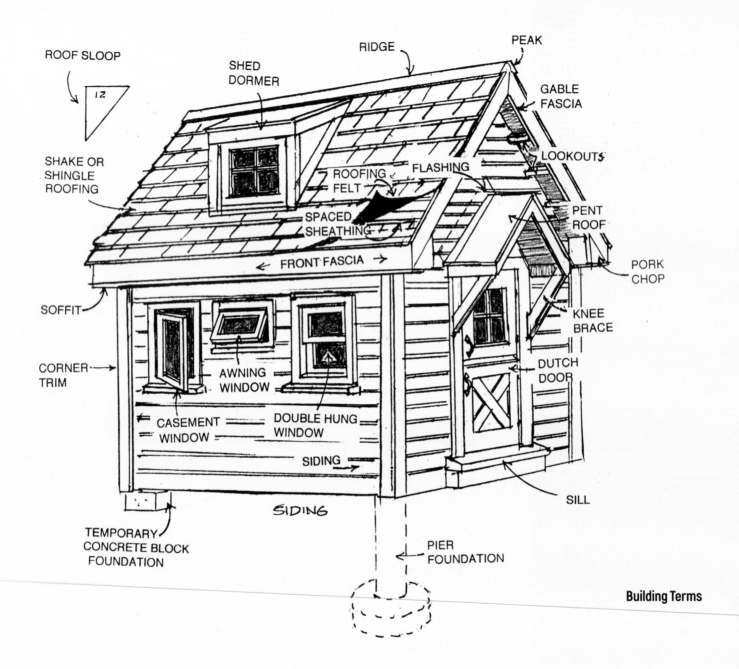

ROOF SLOOP

12

SHAKE OR
SHINGLE
ROOFING

SHED
DORMER

RIDGE

PEAK

GABLE
FASCIA

LOOKOUTS

ROOFING
FELT

FLASHING

SPACED
SHEATHING

PENT
ROOF

PORK
CHOP

FRONT FASCIA

SOFFIT

KNEE
BRACE

CORNER
TRIM

AWNING
WINDOW

DUTCH
DOOR

CASEMENT
WINDOW

DOUBLE HUNG
WINDOW

SIDING

SILL

SIDING

TEMPORARY
CONCRETE BLOCK
FOUNDATION

PIER
FOUNDATION

Building Terms

general building information

PLANNING

Regardless of what you are using your tiny house for, light is an important consideration. The structure's orientation to the sun determines how much light will enter. Would you like sunlight to be streaming in the windows in the morning or in the evening? Do you prefer indirect lighting? Trees are a good way to shade a building from direct sun and can also help to block a northern wind. Keep in mind that prevailing winds change direction slightly from summer to winter. If your house or studio is in the northern region of North America you might want to position it so that the wind strikes the most protected side where there are no doors or windows. On the other hand, if you live in the south, you might position your house to catch cool breezes. Also, position it so that the front door won't catch the wind and blow open, but rather so that the prevailing winds will push it closed. If you have a large, wooded lot, you may want your house tucked away behind some trees, but consider how you will be transporting building materials to your site before finalizing that decision. Are there any gates or fences that you will have to get through? Can a delivery truck reach your site without driving over flower beds or underground irrigation systems? Are there any power lines or low hanging branches that might get in the way of a large delivery truck?

If you plan to use your small house as a home office or studio adjacent to your main house, consider how far you are willing to walk from your main house to reach the studio. Will it be near enough to run an electric line to?

NEIGHBORS & COMMUNITIES

Will your neighbors object if you build your structure next to their side windows? Will they object to the noise while you are building it? Will they complain about the style or color of your house? It is usually a good idea to show a sketch of the building to your neighbors before beginning construction. You might even ask for their suggestions to get them enthusiastic about the idea. You don't have to follow their suggestions, just listen to them. (We are told that in Japan a contractor visits everyone in the community before construction and offers them his apologies and a box of cookies.) If you are part of a homeowners association, check to see if they have restrictions that would affect your plans to build a small structure. If your community has an architectural review board or a historical preservation society, they may require you to submit plans for their approval.

PERMITS

In some communities in the United States you are not required to have a building permit if the building is under 100 square feet and not attached to a permanent foundation so it can be moved later. However, it is always a good idea to check with your local building department before taking out a hammer and saw. If you need a permit, go to your local building department with a copy of your survey and show them where you plan to build. The building department will want to know if you plan to run electricity or plumbing lines to your structure. If you intend to have running water and a toilet you will need to submit an application to your local health department. This can take several weeks – even months – to receive and involves more paperwork and inspections. A building department wants to make sure you are clear about the usage of your small structure – a house, a workshop, a studio and a guest house may all have different requirements. They may suspect that someone is pretending to build a "workshop" which could later be rented out to tenants. You may not be allowed to build near any environmentally restricted areas, such as protected wetlands. Building on or near wetlands always requires special permits, variances and inspections – so allow for extra time.

TOOLS

You may need to invest in a few tools if you are building your own structure. At the very least you will need a portable electric, circular saw to make cuts; however, you will be able to work a lot faster and more accurately if you have a compound miter saw and a contractor's table saw to make rip cuts. An electric jigsaw is also useful and a cordless VSR drill is indispensable. It's a good idea to have two of these – keep one charging while you are using the other one. Tools have not escalated in price like other things in our economy and are a good long-term investment.

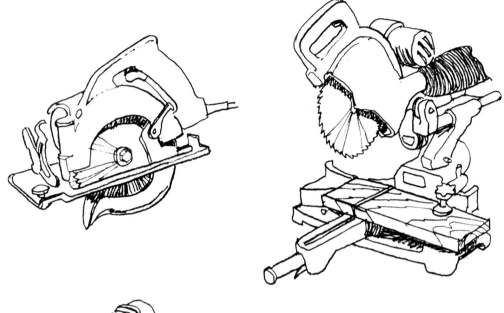

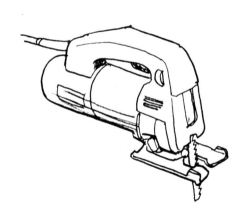

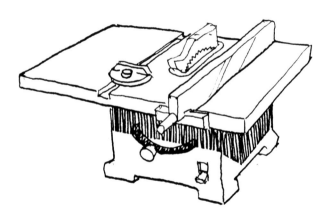

Shown above (clockwise): circular saw, miter saw, table saw, cordless drill, jigsaw.

SCREWS

We recommend using screws, rather than nails, wherever possible. Screws hold much better than nails and can be removed more easily if you make a mistake. Another good reason for using them is that the force of hammering in a nail can dislodge some of the framing you have previously put together and knock those perfect joints out of square. Although screws cost more than nails, we find that they are well worth the extra cost.

We prefer star-drive deck screws because the drill bit is less likely to slip off the screw head. If you are over 50 years old, you may still have slotted-head screws (get rid of them!) or the more recent Phillips-head screws. Although stainless steel screws are more resistant to salt water, they are softer steel and the heads can "strip" making it almost impossible to remove if necessary. Use square-drive screws if you already have them but try to stick with one type or the other, as it is a nuisance to keep changing bits. Many of the new types of screws come with a free drill bit in the package to fit that type of screw. At the time of writing, no manufacturer has produced a double-ended bit for both square drive and star drive.

The companion to the screw is of course the screw gun or a quarter-inch drill with a screw bit in its chuck. We find battery-operated drills to be indispensable for big jobs as you avoid dragging around an extension cord while you are working.

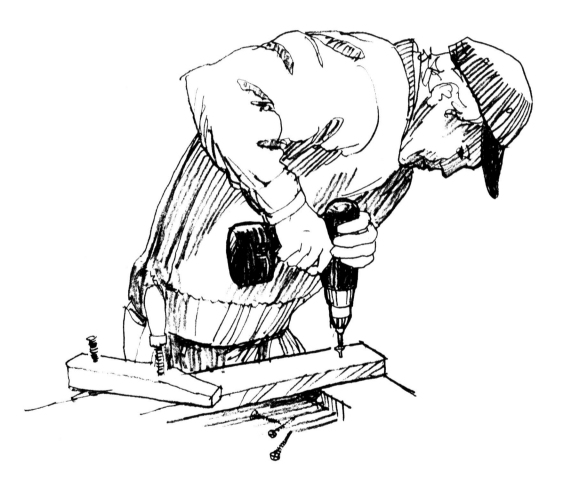

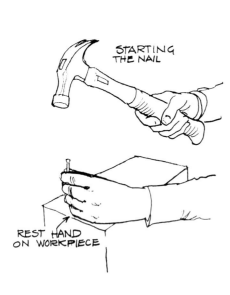

STARTING
THE NAIL

STRIKE
ZONE

REST HAND
ON WORKPIECE

HANDLE
PARALLEL

Proper hammering technique will save you time and energy.

NAILS

Nails are good for specific jobs such as joist hangers, flooring, siding and shingling. Make sure any nail you use is galvanized to prevent rust.

For more power, hold the hammer near the end of the handle and direct your blows so that the lower center face (strike zone) of the hammerhead hits the nail. As in tennis, this is the sweet spot and delivers more bang for the buck.

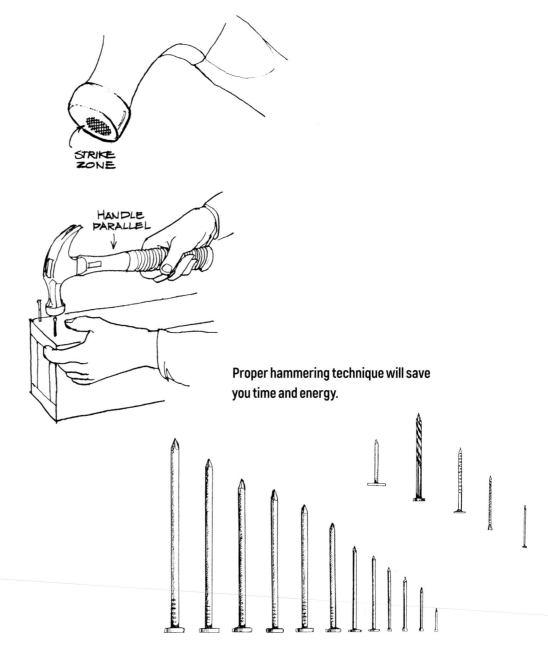

SAWING CROSS-CUT

We recommend that you borrow or buy an electric miter saw (chop saw) for cross cutting. This makes cutting the lumber fast, easy and accurate and allows you to make micro-adjustments, which would be almost impossible using a portable circular saw or handsaw.

Build a stand to support the saw at a convenient height (about 30") and an extension platform to support the long, 12' boards.

Keep the miter saw protected and dry with a plastic contractor bag when not in use.

SAW GUIDE

If you need to cut a sheet of plywood lengthwise and don't have a table saw, a good alternative is to make a guide for a hand-held circular saw. This will enable you to cut a perfectly straight line. The saw guide is made from two strips cut from an 8' long piece of ½" plywood. The first piece (called a fence) is 3" wide and the second piece is 3" wide plus the distance from the inside of the saw blade to the outside of the saw base. Use the "factory edge" of the plywood for the fence to ensure that it is straight; cut the baseboard wider than you need and then glue and nail it to the fence. Using the fence as a guide, trim the baseboard to size with the circular saw.

To use the saw guide, clamp or nail it (using finishing nails) to the sheet of plywood to be cut. Always hold the saw firmly against the fence while making the cut.

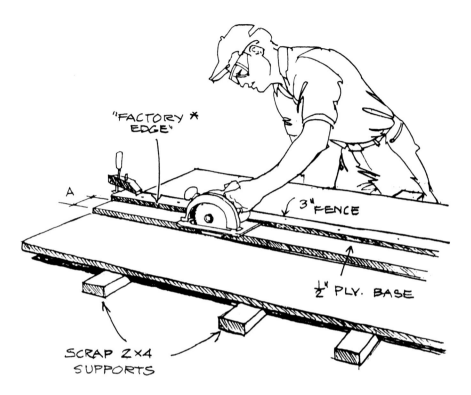

"FACTORY ★ EDGE"

A

3" FENCE

½" PLY. BASE

SCRAP 2×4 SUPPORTS

★ "Factory edge" refers to the outside edge of the plywood as it comes from the factory and is guaranteed to be straight.

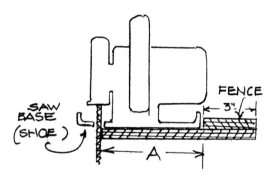

SAW BASE (SHOE)

FENCE

3"

A

STAKING OUT CORNERS FOR A SMALL HOUSE FOOTPRINT

Make your own stakes by cutting four 2x2 posts at various lengths. Cut points on one end of each stake using a hatchet or table saw so that you can drive the stakes into the ground easily. You will be glad you did this later on, when you have to reposition them!

At the highest corner on your building site, pound in the shortest stake. Measure off the length and the width and place a stake at each point. You may want to align your building with another feature on your property (such as a fence or another building). Make the two lines as close as possible to a right angle by "eyeballing" them. To ensure that the two lines are at true right angles, measure the two diagonals, which should be equal. You can also use this tip when you are framing doors and windows.

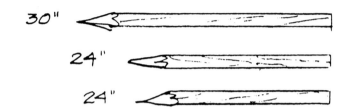

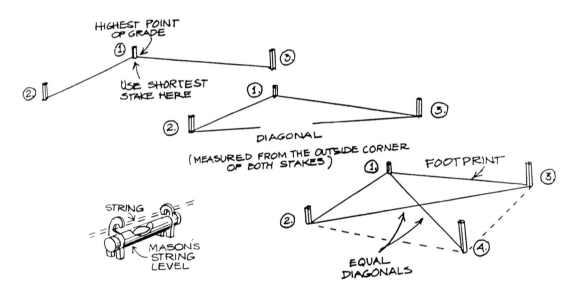

FOUNDATIONS

The simplest and quickest foundation you can make for a small building is to rest it on 8" x 8" x 16" concrete blocks. Since very few building sites are absolutely flat and level, you might also have to use some half blocks (18" x 16" x 4" high). Starting with the highest corner of your building site, bury a block so that it is level with the ground. To prevent settling of your building later on, compact the soil well before placing the block in the hole. Place blocks in the other three corners so that they are level with the top of the first block. Micro adjustments in the heights of the blocks can be made by shimming with thin pieces of slate or even tabs of asphalt roofing.

Post & Skirt Permanent Foundation

If your building requires a permanent foundation, you can build a post and skirt foundation quickly and inexpensively. This type of foundation is ideal for building in remote locations, where it may be impractical to bring in heavy machinery to excavate. The design diverts rainwater away from the foundation (helping to prevent frost heave), and captures geothermal heat rising from the ground. Also, by lining the interior with rigid insulation you can achieve a higher "R" value than if using standard concrete blocks or a poured foundation.

In some regions of the United States, building laws require that a foundation have a masonry perimeter; since this design has a cement board around its base, it may be permissible. Check your local codes.

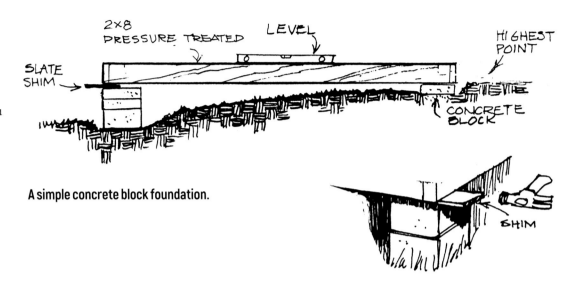

A simple concrete block foundation.

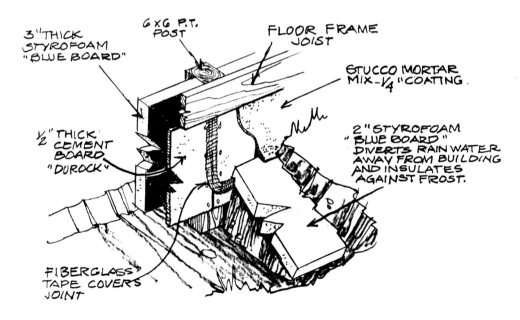

A post and skirt design can divert rainwater water away from your foundation.

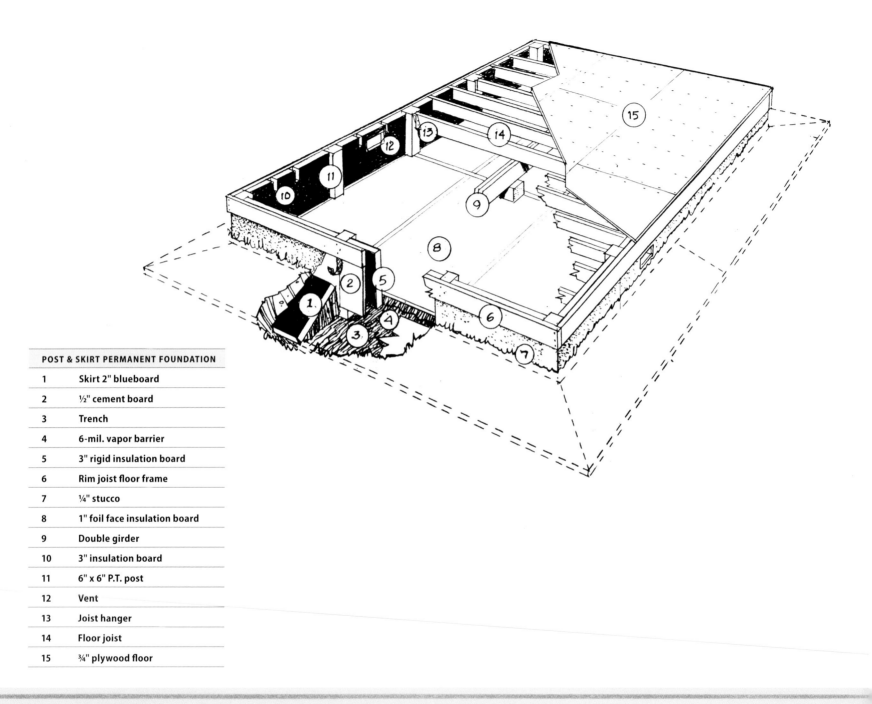

POST & SKIRT PERMANENT FOUNDATION

1	Skirt 2" blueboard
2	½" cement board
3	Trench
4	6-mil. vapor barrier
5	3" rigid insulation board
6	Rim joist floor frame
7	¼" stucco
8	1" foil face insulation board
9	Double girder
10	3" insulation board
11	6" x 6" P.T. post
12	Vent
13	Joist hanger
14	Floor joist
15	¾" plywood floor

FRAMING & TRIMMING A WINDOW

In preparation for the window sashes you need to make a frame (window jamb) and a pressure-treated sill to hold it in place. Start by cutting a piece of 2x6 pressure-treated wood, 6" wider than the window. (This allows for the side jambs and casings.) Rip-cut the two long edges of the 2x6 to a 10° angle to create the drainage slope. Make a ⅛" dado cut on the bottom of the sill to provide a drip edge for rain. Cut a 4¼" x 3" notch in each end and set the sill in the rough opening using shims on the inside. Nail a 1x3 to the sill on the inside of the building. This covers the gap and keeps the window in place.

Build the window frame (jambs) using 1x6 boards ripped down to 4½"; cut the bottom of the side jambs at 10° to match the slope of the sill. The window opening allows for ¼" wiggle room on each side. Insert tapered shims (wood shingles) into the gaps for final adjustments. Nail a ½" x 1¼" stop to the inside of the window frame to hold the window and eliminate draughts.

Make the trim (casing) by rip-cutting a 1x6 board in half, making each piece 2⅝" wide. For a neat appearance, make the head casing overlap the two side casings by ⅜".

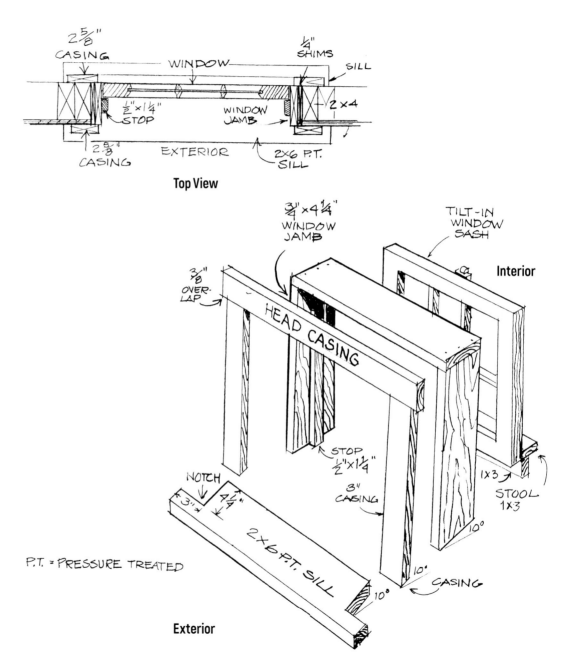

Top View

Exterior

P.T. = PRESSURE TREATED

LOFT WINDOW

A small window – for instance, a window in a loft – is not difficult to make. If you have a table saw, it can be done in less than half an hour. From an 8' (1½" x 2½") piece of cedar or mahogany, cut two pieces 19¼" long (stiles) and two pieces 18¼" long (rails). Cut a ⅜" x ⅝" rabbet along the edge of each piece as shown in the profile detail. (Save the leftover pieces for later.) Clamp the two longer pieces (stiles) together and cut a 2½" shoulder notch out of the ends. Locate the center of all four pieces and cut a ⅝" x ⅝" dado for the muntins. From the leftover wood, cut two ⅝" x ⅝" muntin bars and cross-notch them in the middle. Glue and screw all the pieces together, and cut a piece of ¹⁄₁₆" glass or Plexiglas to fit the rabbet. Cut the ends of the leftover pieces at a 45° angle and fit them into the rabbets to hold the glass in place. On your table saw, trim the bottom edge of the window at 10° to match the slope of the sill.

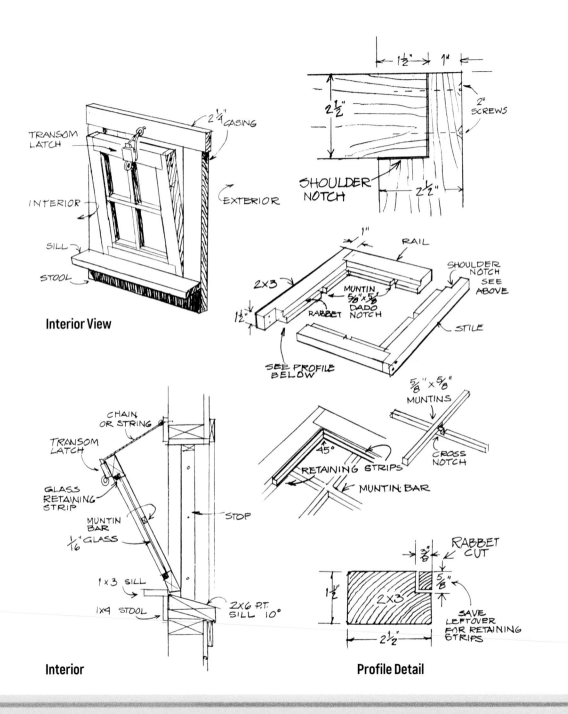

Interior View

Interior

Profile Detail

SCREENS

Make your own screens, using lightweight
1x3 boards (preferably red cedar). Cut four
pieces of 1x3 to fit the opening. Using a
table saw, cut a ⅛" wide x ¼" deep groove,
⅜" from the inside edge of all four pieces.
Cut the lap joints on the table saw. Join the
pieces together using galvanized brads and
waterproof glue. Once the glue has dried, cut
a piece of insect screen 1" larger on all sides
than the inside opening. Lay the screening
over the frame and, using a tool made especially for this purpose, press the screen and a
retaining spline into the groove. Trim off any
excess screening with a utility knife.

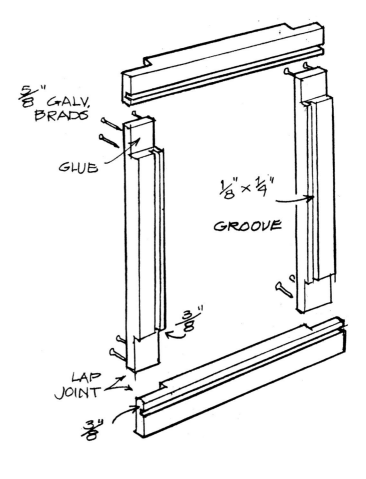

⅝" GALV. BRADS

GLUE

⅛" x ¼" GROOVE

⅜"

LAP JOINT

⅜"

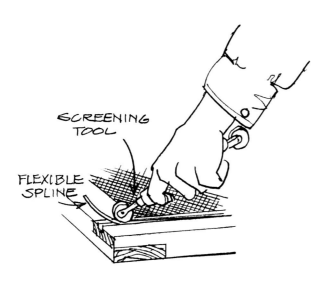

SCREENING TOOL

FLEXIBLE SPLINE

SKYLIGHTS

Skylights admit 30% more light than windows and save electricity. Factory-built skylights cost around $300, but you can make one yourself for under $100.

Standing inside your building, use a framing square to locate and mark where you want the corners of the skylight. It must be located between two rafters. Reinforce the top and bottom of the proposed skylight with cross-headers between the rafters.

Build a "curb" frame with 2x4s above the rafters and the headers, that protrudes about 2" above the surface of the roof. Caulk around the curb where it meets the roof.

To seal the skylight, install 8" wide x 10" tall aluminum flashing. Working from the bottom up, bend each piece as shown, laying one side against the curb and the other against the roof. Overlap each piece of flashing and staple it to the roof, placing the staple at the top edge so that the next layer covers the staple. Cover the top edge of the skylight with a single piece of flashing, cut and bent as shown. The roof shingles will later cover this.

Cut a piece of ¼" Plexiglas (acrylic) 1" longer than the skylight curb, and drill ¼" holes 6" apart along the two sides and the top edge (but not along the bottom edge). Lay a strip of glazing tape around the top edge of the curb, and lay the Plexiglas over it so 1" overlaps the bottom. Using rubber washers and #8, 1" pan-head screws, attach the Plexiglas to the curb. Be careful not to over-tighten the screws or they may crack the plastic. The oversize pilot holes that you drilled will allow for contraction and expansion during temperature changes.

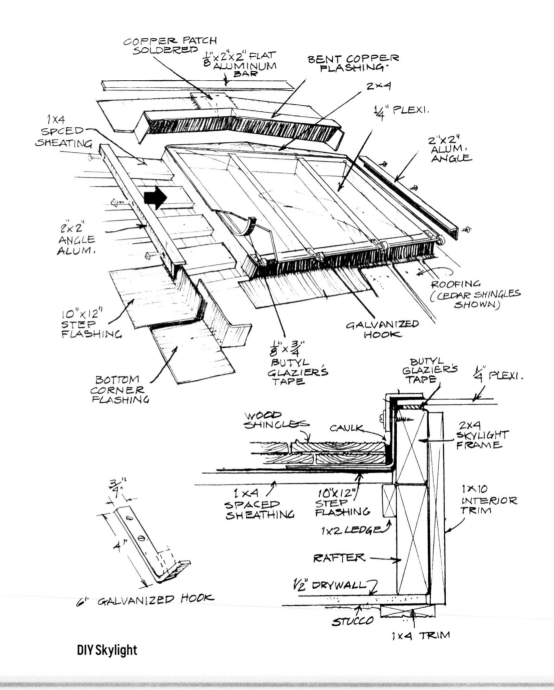

DIY Skylight

Finish the skylight by installing brown, aluminum drip edge along the sides and top to protect the screw holes. Lay a generous bead of caulk before attaching the drip edge. Use only four screws through the side corners to hold the drip edge in place. Notice that the top piece of drip edge goes on last and overlaps the sides.

To keep the plexiglas from slipping down, buy ¾" x 5" galvanized "mending" plates and use a vise to bend them into a "U" shape at the bottom. Drill two ⅛" holes in the top end of the plates and screw them to the bottom curb.

MOVING TINY HOUSES

There are several ways to move a small structure. The easiest is to hire someone with a front-end loader to drive it to the desired location. However, if you are feeling adventurous, you might try moving it yourself using this technique:

Buy three 10' long 5" diameter poles from a fencing outlet. Using car or house jacks, raise the building and place two, long 2x4s under it, in the direction of the move, to act as rails. Lay two of the poles under the structure on top of the rails and the third pole in front to catch it as it rolls forward. Dig a 2'-deep hole in the ground and bury a boat anchor in it with the shank poking up above ground. Tie a strong rope around the building and through a pulley. Get several strong volunteers to help you pull on the rope or attach it to a truck. Pull the house slowly, removing the poles from the rear and placing them in the front as you go along. If you are moving the house downhill, place the anchor on the uphill side and use the rope and pulley as a brake instead.

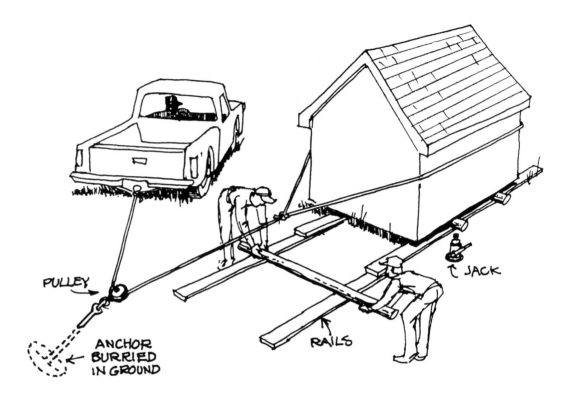

PULLEY

ANCHOR BURRIED IN GROUND

JACK

RAILS

ONE | building small houses

the versatile tiny house

This tiny 10' x 12' house is an ideal size for minimal living and encapsulates the theme of this book: it's a comfortable space for two people to live, work or play in. We've been designing small buildings for many years and have found these dimensions especially versatile. This design includes a space-saving loft (with a small window) for sleeping or storage, plenty of windows on the ground floor, and the option of a skylight if even more light is desired. We've suggested some alternative interior plans, or you can adapt it to your needs and dreams.

This house is built using conventional 2x4 construction methods, but can easily be modified with sustainable living in mind. For example, a metal or corrugated plastic roof will allow you to collect rain water, and solar panels will generate power for electric light, radio and a computer. There is room for a fold-out double bed downstairs, in addition to the 4' x 8' loft space. A wood-burning stove provides heating and cooking facilities; it can be moved outside in the summer to help keep the interior cool.

The sturdy front door is hinged to swing outwards, for strength and to save interior space. The window frames are made from recycled milk bottles; they look like traditional wooden frames but far outlast them and are maintenance-free. They tilt inwards for ventilation and cleaning, and can be fitted with screens in the summer or clear energy panels in the winter.

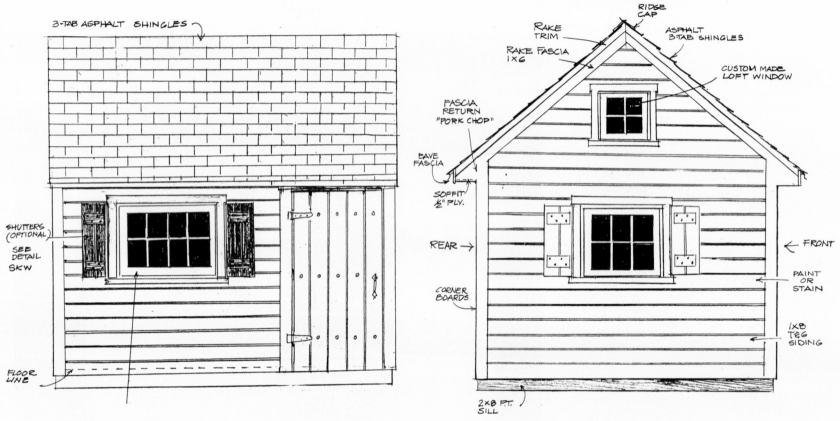

3-TAB ASPHALT SHINGLES

RIDGE CAP

RAKE TRIM

RAKE FASCIA 1X6

ASPHALT 3-TAB SHINGLES

CUSTOM MADE LOFT WINDOW

FASCIA RETURN "PORK CHOP"

EAVE FASCIA

SOFFIT ½" PLY.

SHUTTERS (OPTIONAL)

SEE DETAIL SKW

REAR

FRONT

PAINT OR STAIN

CORNER BOARDS

1X8 T&G SIDING

FLOOR LINE

2X8 P.T. SILL

✱ WINDOW 42"x29"
RECYCLED PRODUCTS CO.
1 800 765 1489

Front View

Side View

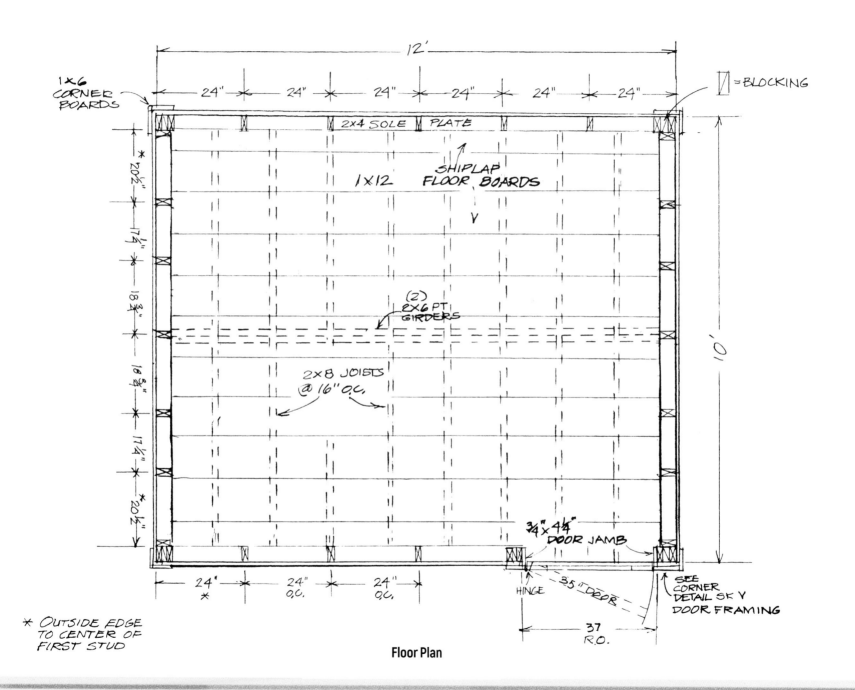

12'

1x6 CORNER BOARDS

⌷ = BLOCKING

24"   24"   24"   24"   24"   24"

2x4 SOLE PLATE

SHIPLAP FLOOR BOARDS

1x12

(2) 2x6 PT GIRDERS

2x8 JOISTS @ 16" O.C.

20½"   17¼"   18¾"   18¾"   17¼"   20½"

10'

¾" x 4¼" DOOR JAMB

HINGE   35" DOOR   37 R.O.

SEE CORNER DETAIL SK Y DOOR FRAMING

24"   24" O.C.   24" O.C.

* OUTSIDE EDGE TO CENTER OF FIRST STUD

Floor Plan

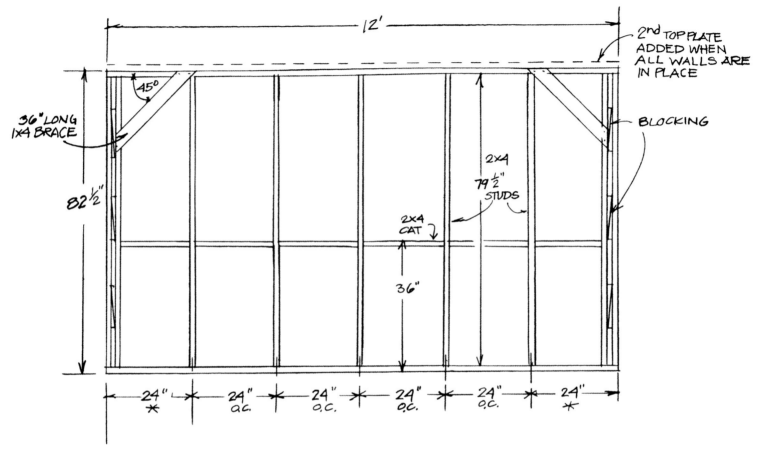

12'

2nd TOP PLATE ADDED WHEN ALL WALLS ARE IN PLACE

45°

36" LONG 1x4 BRACE

BLOCKING

2x4 79½" STUDS

82½"

2x4 CAT

36"

24" *

24" O.C.

24" O.C.

24" O.C.

24" O.C.

24" *

* OUTSIDE EDGE TO CENTER OF FIRST STUD

O.C. = ON CENTER

Back Wall
(as viewed from interior)

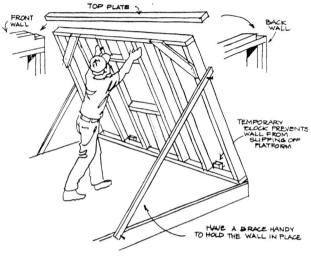

CUT A SECOND TOP PLATE LONGER SO IT OVERLAPS THE FRONT AND BACK WALLS LOCKING THEM TOGETHER:

TOP PLATE

FRONT WALL

BACK WALL

TEMPORARY BLOCK PREVENTS WALL FROM SLIPPING OFF PLATFORM

HAVE A BRACE HANDY TO HOLD THE WALL IN PLACE

Raising the shed walls

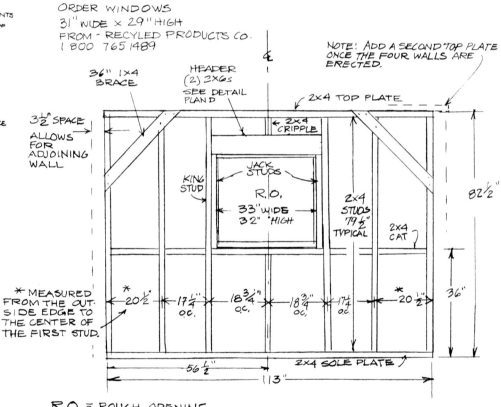

ORDER WINDOWS
31" WIDE × 29" HIGH
FROM - RECYCLED PRODUCTS CO.
1 800 765 1489

NOTE: ADD A SECOND TOP PLATE ONCE THE FOUR WALLS ARE ERECTED.

36" 1×4 BRACE

HEADER (2) 2×6s SEE DETAIL PLAN D

2×4 TOP PLATE

2×4 CRIPPLE

$3\frac{1}{2}$" SPACE ALLOWS FOR ADJOINING WALL

KING STUD

JACK STUDS

R.O. 33" WIDE 32" HIGH

2×4 STUDS $79\frac{1}{2}$" TYPICAL

2×4 CAT

$82\frac{1}{2}$"

36"

* MEASURED FROM THE OUT SIDE EDGE TO THE CENTER OF THE FIRST STUD.

* $20\frac{1}{2}$" $17\frac{1}{4}$" O.C. $18\frac{3}{4}$" O.C. $18\frac{3}{4}$" O.C. $17\frac{1}{4}$" O.C. * $20\frac{1}{2}$"

$56\frac{1}{2}$"

2×4 SOLE PLATE

113"

R.O. = ROUGH OPENING

O.C. = ON CENTER

℄ = CENTER LINE

NOTE: FOLLOW SAME FRAMING ON OPPOSITE WALL.

Side Wall Frame

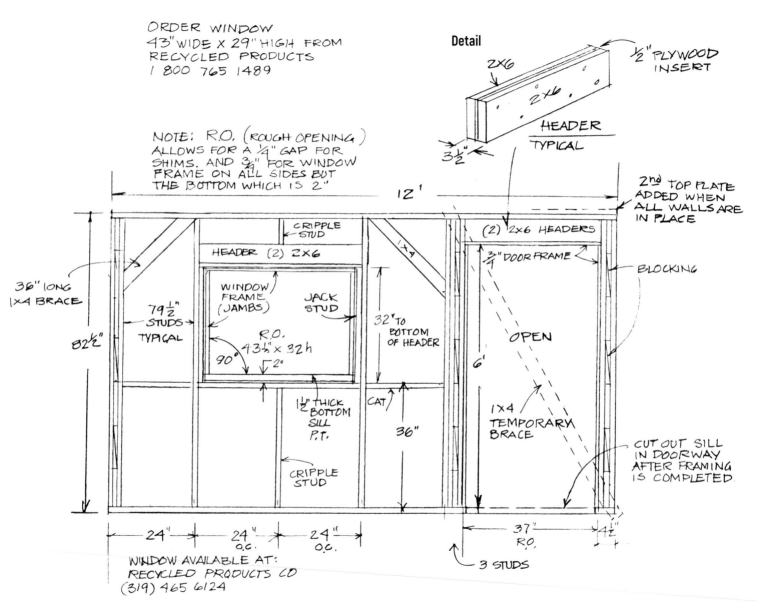

ORDER WINDOW
43" WIDE x 29" HIGH FROM
RECYCLED PRODUCTS
1 800 765 1489

NOTE: R.O. (ROUGH OPENING)
ALLOWS FOR A 1/4" GAP FOR
SHIMS. AND 3/4" FOR WINDOW
FRAME ON ALL SIDES BUT
THE BOTTOM WHICH IS 2"

Detail

2X6

2X6

2X6

1/2" PLYWOOD
INSERT

HEADER
TYPICAL

3 1/2"

12'

2nd TOP PLATE
ADDED WHEN
ALL WALLS ARE
IN PLACE

CRIPPLE
STUD

HEADER (2) 2X6

(2) 2X6 HEADERS

3/4" DOOR FRAME

BLOCKING

36" LONG
1X4 BRACE

82 1/2"

79 1/2"
STUDS
TYPICAL

WINDOW
FRAME
(JAMBS)

JACK
STUD

1X4

R.O.
43 1/2" x 32h

90°

2"

32" TO
BOTTOM
OF HEADER

OPEN

6'

1X4
TEMPORARY
BRACE

1 1/2" THICK
BOTTOM
SILL
P.T.

CAT

36"

CRIPPLE
STUD

CUT OUT SILL
IN DOORWAY
AFTER FRAMING
IS COMPLETED.

24"

24"
O.C.

24"
O.C.

37"
R.O.

4 1/2"

3 STUDS

WINDOW AVAILABLE AT:
RECYCLED PRODUCTS CO
(319) 465 6124

Front Wall Frame
(exterior view)

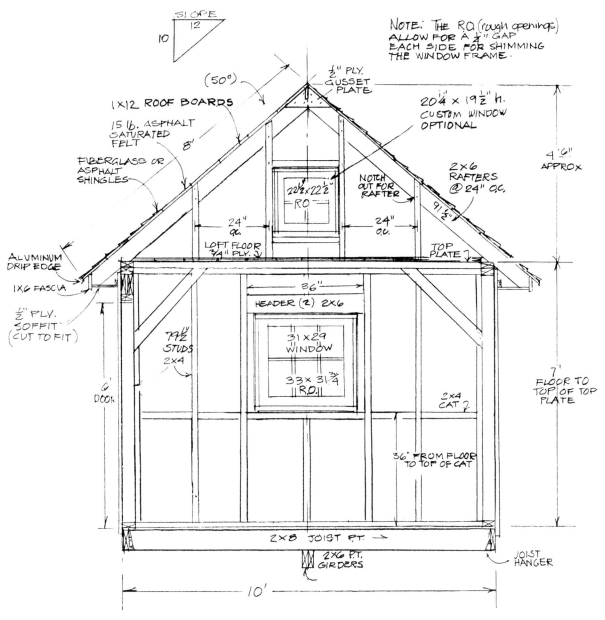

SLOPE 10/12

NOTE: THE R.O. (rough openings) ALLOW FOR A 1/4" GAP EACH SIDE FOR SHIMMING THE WINDOW FRAME.

1/2" PLY. GUSSET PLATE

1X12 ROOF BOARDS

(50°)

20 1/4 x 19 1/2" h. CUSTOM WINDOW OPTIONAL

15 lb. ASPHALT SATURATED FELT

8'

FIBERGLASS OR ASPHALT SHINGLES

22 1/2 x 22 1/2" R.O.

NOTCH OUT FOR RAFTER

2x6 RAFTERS @ 24" O.C.

9' 1/2"

24" O.C.

24" O.C.

TOP PLATE

ALUMINUM DRIP EDGE

LOFT FLOOR 3/4" PLY.

4' 6" APPROX

1X6 FASCIA

36"

HEADER (2) 2x6

1/2" PLY. SOFFIT (CUT TO FIT)

79 1/2" STUDS 2x4

31 x 29 WINDOW

33 x 31 3/4 R.O.

2x4 CAT

6' DOOR

36" FROM FLOOR TO TOP OF CAT

7' FLOOR TO TOP OF TOP PLATE

2x8 JOIST P.T. →

JOIST HANGER

2x6 P.T. GIRDERS

10'

Cross Section

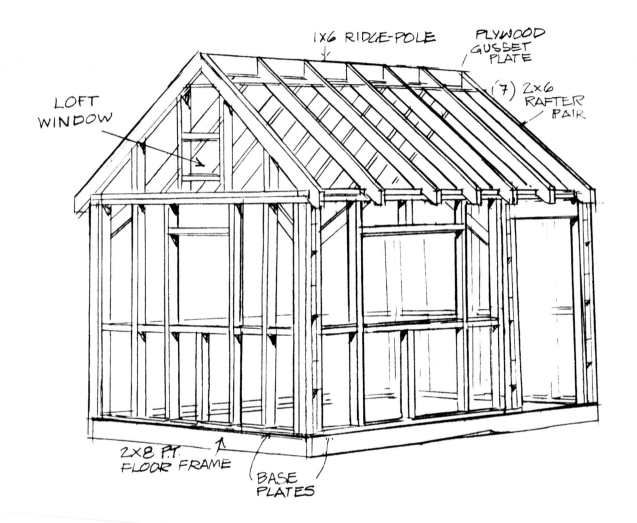

1X6 RIDGE-POLE

PLYWOOD GUSSET PLATE

(7) 2X6 RAFTER PAIR

LOFT WINDOW

2X8 P.T. FLOOR FRAME

BASE PLATES

Framing

MATERIALS

Qty.	Description	Size	Location
FOUNDATION			
4	Concrete blocks	3" x 8" x 16"	foundation
FLOOR			
2	2x8 P.T.	10'	floor frame
2	2x8 P.T.	12'	floor frame
2	2x6 P.T.	12'	girder (opt.)
8	2x8 P.T.	10'	floor joists
12	1x12 shiplap #2 pine	12'	flooring
WALL FRAMING			
2	2x4 #2 const. grade fir	8'	props
17	2x4 #2 const. grade fir	14'	studs (vertical timbers)
6	2x4 #2 const. grade fir	10'	side plates
6	2x4 #2 const. grade fir	12'	front & rear plates
2	2x4 #2 const. grade fir	16'	cats (horizontal timbers)
3	2x4 #2 const. grade fir3	12'	jack studs, blocks & mast
3	1x4 #2 pine	12'	braces
GABLE FRAMING			
3	2x4 #2 const. grade fir	12'	gables
HEADERS			
2	2x6 #2 const. grade fir	10'	windows & door
SIDING			
8	1x8 T&G V-groove #2 pine	12'	rear wall
6	1x8 T&G V-groove #2 pine	8'	front wall
12	1x8 T&G V-groove #2 pine	10'	side walls
6	1x8 T&G V-groove #2 pine	14'	side gables

ROOF

1	1x4 #2 pine	12'	ridge board
14	2x6 #2 const. grade fir	8'	rafters
18	1x12 shiplap #2 pine	12'	roof boards
1	15 lb. asphalt felt	36" roll	underlayment
3	Alum. brown eave drip edge	10'	eaves
4	Alum. brown rake drip edge	10'	rakes
6	bundles 3-tab asphalt shingles		roof

TRIM

2	1x6 #2 const. pine	14'	eave fascias
4	1x6 #2 const. pine	8'	rake fascias
4	1x2 #2 pine	8'	rake trim
2	¾" x ¾" quarter-round	12'	soffit trim
5	1x6 #2 pine	14'	corner boards & left door trim

WINDOWS

2	barn sashes Recycled Prods.	31" x 29"	
1	barn sash Recycled Prods.	42" x 29"	
3	1x6 clear cedar	10'	window frames
1	2x6 P.T.	14'	window sills
2	1x2 #2 pine	8'	window trim
3	transom latches		window

DOOR

3	1x8 T&G V-groove #2 pine	14'	door
2	1x2 #2 pine	12'	stop & sill strip

MISCELLANEOUS

1	½" AC Plywood	4' x 8'	gusset plates, soffit, & header inserts.
3	exterior latex paint	3 gals.	exterior walls

HARDWARE			
1	joist hanger nails	box	floor joists
1	3½"common galv. nails	2 lbs.	floor
2	3" galvanized finishing nails	3 lbs.	siding
2	3" star drive coated screws	2 lbs.	frame
18	¼" x 1¾" galv. carriage bolts		door
2	6" galv. strap hinges		door
1	gate latch		door
1	1½" galvanized finishing nails	1 box	mouldings
2	1" wide head shingle nails	2 lbs.	asphalt shingle roof
4	transom latches		

FLOOR FRAMING

Cut two pieces of 2x8 pressure-treated lumber 11' 9" long for the front and back floor frames, and two pieces 10' long for the side floor frames. (The back and front pieces are shorter than the final length of the house to allow for the two 1½" thick side floor frames.) Assemble them as a 10' x 12' rectangle on the blocks, and nail them together with four 3½" galvanized nails at each corner.

Girder (optional)

To strengthen the floor, place two 12' long 2x6 P.T. boards (nailed together) under the middle of the house floor. Depending on your building site, you may have to dig and/or add support such as compacted dirt, rocks or concrete blocks to make the girder level with the bottom of the floor joists.

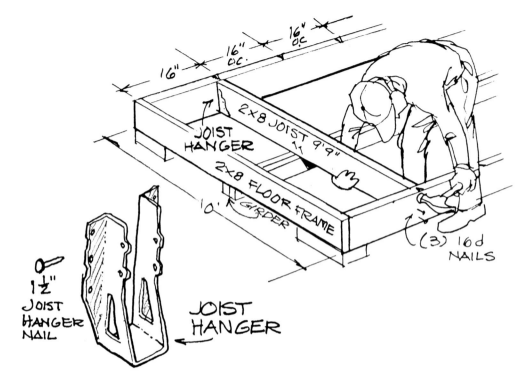

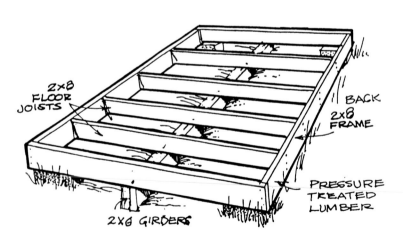

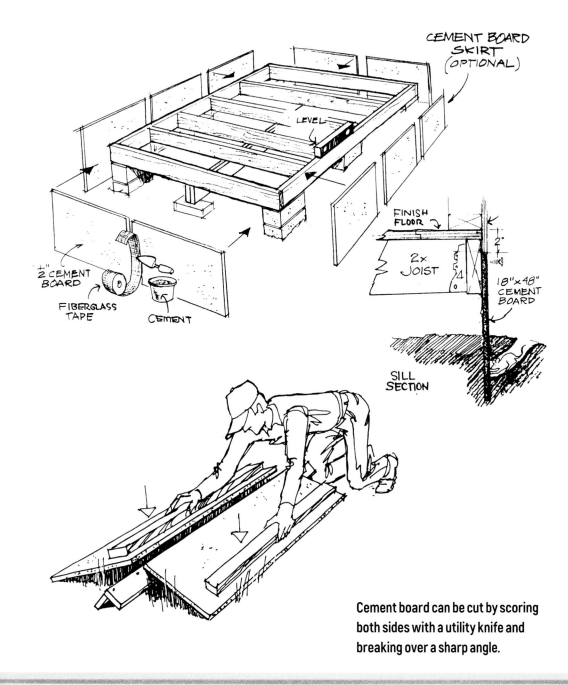

CEMENT BOARD
SKIRT
(OPTIONAL)

LEVEL

½" CEMENT
BOARD

FIBERGLASS
TAPE

CEMENT

FINISH
FLOOR

2x
JOIST

18"x48"
CEMENT
BOARD

SILL
SECTION

Cement board can be cut by scoring both sides with a utility knife and breaking over a sharp angle.

Place a mark at 16" intervals along both 12' sides of the floor frame, and cut eight pieces of 2x8 P.T. lumber 9' 9" long. Nail metal joist hangers at each 16" mark. (Use special joist hanger nails.) Slip the joists into the pockets of the hangers, and toenail (nail at an angle) through each joist and into the center girder as well.

This type of corner block foundation is considered "temporary," and makes it possible to move the building if the need arises. To keep out wind, drifting leaves and small animals, attach 18" x 48" panels of ½" cement board around the perimeter of the house. Score both sides of the cement board with a utility knife and snap it over a sharp edge. Dig a trench around the shed, deep enough for the cement board to rest below ground and with its top edge 2" below the top of the floor frame. Use screws especially made for cement board to attach it to the frame. Cover the joints of the cement board with fiberglass tape, and plaster the entire surface with cement/sand mix. When the cement has cured – usually within a day – backfill the trench with soil.

FLOORING

We used economical #2 pine boards. They are easy to carry, have an aromatic smell of the northern pine forests, and leave little waste. Leftover pieces can easily be split with a hatchet and used as kindling.

If you require an especially sturdy building, you could use 1x12 shiplap cladding on the walls, and 2x6 or 2x8 tongue and groove fir or southern pine flooring. Blind nail at an angle.

Installing the floorboards is not difficult. Install the first board with the lip on the bottom and face-nail the board to the joists. Spread a bead of PL 400 construction adhesive on top of the joists and use 3" galvanized finishing nails to face-nail the boards. Use a nail set to sink the nail heads 1/16" below the surface.

WALL FRAMING

Start the back wall frame by cutting two 12' 2x4 pieces for the bottom (sole plate) and the top plate. (You will be adding a second top plate later to tie the walls together.) Use the floor that you have just completed to lay out the pieces to be nailed together. Cut nine 2x4 studs 79½" long and assemble them as shown. Measure and mark along the 2x4 plates at 24" intervals and nail them to the studs using two 3½" nails at each joint. The two end posts consist of two studs with three 18" 2x4 blocks spaced between them. This will allow for a 1" nailing surface in case you decide to finish off the interior with drywall or paneling. Measure the diagonals of the completed wall to make sure they are equal and nail 1x4 braces onto the top corners to keep the wall square. Cut

the 1x4 corner braces 36" long and miter the ends at 45°, then nail them to the top plate and the end stud. Set them into the studs and plates if you plan to finish the interior.

To raise the rear wall frame, temporarily nail a 2x4 to the outside of each end stud. These will act as braces until you add the adjoining side walls. To keep the wall frame from slipping off the edge of the floor while

you raise it, temporarily screw three short blocks to the floor frame.

Lift the wall frame up in place, check the vertical with a level and temporarily nail the bottom of the 2x4 braces to the floor frame. Raise the other three walls the same way.

Add another layer of 2x4s, with overlapping joints at the corners.

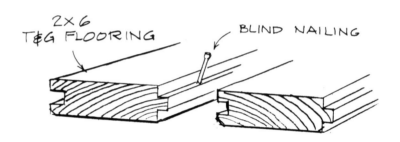

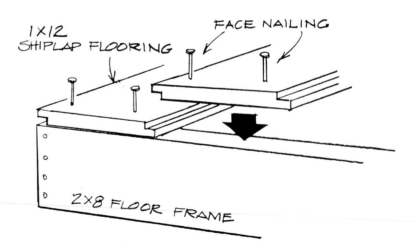

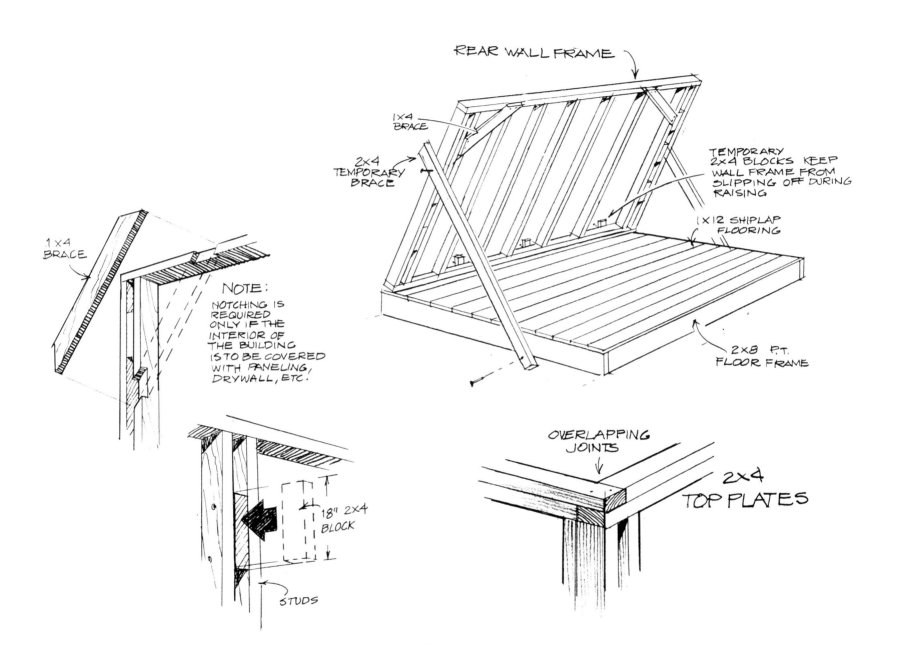

REAR WALL FRAME

1×4 BRACE

2×4 TEMPORARY BRACE

TEMPORARY 2×4 BLOCKS KEEP WALL FRAME FROM SLIPPING OFF DURING RAISING

1×12 SHIPLAP FLOORING

2×8 P.T. FLOOR FRAME

1×4 BRACE

NOTE:
NOTCHING IS REQUIRED ONLY IF THE INTERIOR OF THE BUILDING IS TO BE COVERED WITH PANELING, DRYWALL, ETC.

18" 2×4 BLOCK

STUDS

OVERLAPPING JOINTS

2×4 TOP PLATES

RAFTERS

You will need fourteen 2x6 rafters spaced 24" apart. Start by cutting 2½" off the end of an 8' 2x6 to make it 93½" long. Following the Rafter Detail shown right, measure up from the bottom edge of the 2x6 and make a mark (see Mark 1). Place a framing square on the mark and adjust it to measure 4¾" to the top edge of the rafter and 2¾" to the bottom edge. Mark this profile and cut off. For the top end of the rafter, measure down 4½" on the end of the rafter and cut off.

A bird's-mouth notch enables the rafter to sit properly on the top plate. Measure up 7⅜" from the bottom edge of the rafter and make a mark (see Mark 2). Again, place the framing square on the mark and adjust it to measure 1½" up and 1⅞" across. Mark and cut the bird's mouth notch using an electric jigsaw. Using this rafter as a guide, mark and cut an identical rafter to make a pair.

Lay the two rafters on the shed floor so that their tops are touching, and place a temporary 10' long 2x4 in the bird's-mouth notches to act as a spacer. To hold the rafters together, temporarily screw a 1x4 across the middle.

To join them together at the top, cut two triangles of ½" plywood, 18½" across the base and 12" on the two other sides. Screw these plywood gussets to the top of the rafters with 1½" screws. Using a jigsaw, cut a 3½" x ¾" slot in the top for the ridge board. Place the pair of rafters on the top plates to check for fit, and adjust the cuts if necessary. Using the first rafter as a guide, mark and cut the rest of the rafters.

To locate where the rafters will go, make a mark at 24" intervals along the top edge of the ridge board. Lay the ridge board down flat on the top wall plates and transfer the marks onto the outside edge of the top plates so that the rafters will rest directly over the wall studs. This will help distribute the weight of the roof directly down to the foundation.

Nail a temporary 12' 2x4 (mast) to the center of the end walls to help stabilize the placement of the rafters in the next step. Starting with the end rafters, lift them into place and screw them to the wall plates. Screw the ridge-board into the two slots and continue adding the remaining rafters.

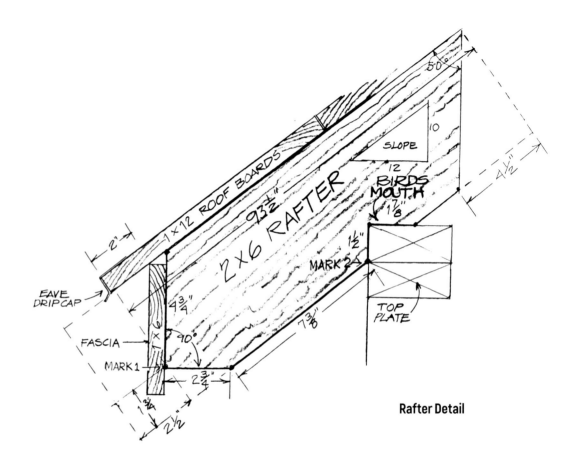

Rafter Detail

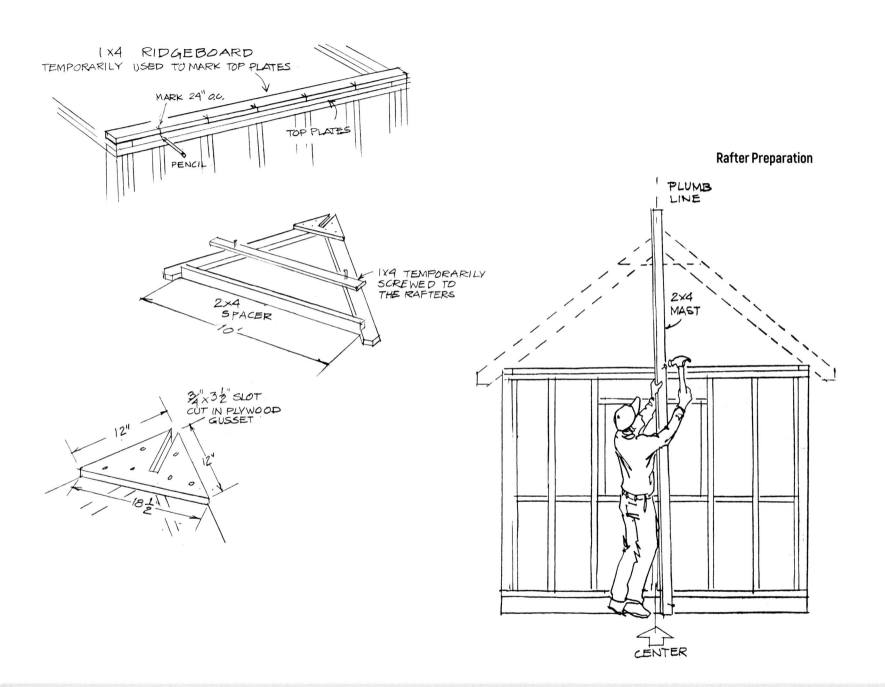

1x4 RIDGEBOARD
TEMPORARILY USED TO MARK TOP PLATES

MARK 24" O.C.

PENCIL

TOP PLATES

Rafter Preparation

PLUMB LINE

2x4 MAST

1x4 TEMPORARILY SCREWED TO THE RAFTERS

2x4 SPACER

10'

$\frac{3}{4}$" x $3\frac{1}{2}$" SLOT CUT IN PLYWOOD GUSSET

12"

12"

$18\frac{1}{2}$"

CENTER

GABLE ENDS

The gable ends are framed in the same way as the walls except that the studs are notched at the top where they meet the end rafters. Start by marking the horizontal center point and measuring over 12" to the left and to the right to mark the center of the first studs. Then measure over another 24" to mark the center of the next studs. This will provide you with framing to nail the siding to and will allow room for a little window that will be greatly appreciated if you use this as a sleeping loft.

ROOF

Installing the roof is fairly simple since the 1x2 shiplap lumber comes in 12' lengths and the building is 12' long. However, double-check the length of each board to see if it is exactly 12' long – many lumber mills leave an extra ½" for damage control.

Since the roof is too steep to walk on, temporarily nail some 2x4 footholds while you attach the boards. You can use the 2x4 masts left over from the previous step.

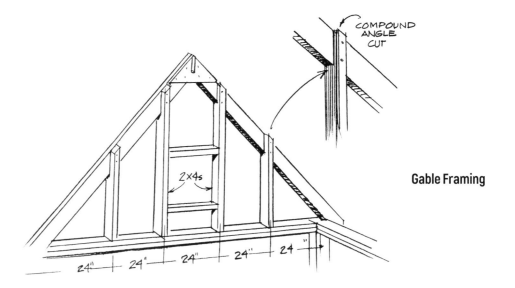

Gable Framing

Roof

SIDING

We chose 1x8 tongue and groove, V-groove horizontal siding for this cabin because it is attractive, easy to install, relatively inexpensive and can be painted or stained any color. If this does not fit your taste, there are plenty of other sidings to choose from. Just keep in mind that if you choose vertical siding, you will need to add more cats on the interior to nail the boards to.

The lowest boards should be back-primed with a rot-preventing sealer, as this is where rainwater will splash up when it falls off the roof. The bottom board should overlap the top 2" of the floor frame. Install the siding with the tongue facing up and the V-groove facing out. Each successive course is nailed through the tongue, at an angle, using 2" galvanized finishing nails. The nail heads will be covered by the next course of tongue and groove boards, to leave an unblemished surface. Use a nail set to drive the nails flush without damaging the boards.

Corner trim will cover ends of the boards later.

TRIM

Cut the two eave fascias from 14' long 1x6 boards, and nail them onto the rafter tails (ends), so they extend 1½" past the ends of the siding on each side.

The 1x6 rake fascias on the sides of the building extend from the peak down to meet the eave fascia (see Side View on page 26). Add a 1x2 rake trim piece to the top edge.

Trim the four corners of the structure with 1x6 #2 pine boards. Note that the corner to the right of the door is a little dif-

ferent. Rip a 1x6 board down to 5¼" to act as a spacer to bring the trim out flush with the casing trim on the left side of the door. The casing boards on either side of the door are 7" wide and overlap the side jambs (see Door Framing sketch below).

Nail a ½" thick plywood soffit to the underside of the rafter ends and hold in place with a ¾" x ¾" strip of quarter-round moulding (see Door Corner Detail on page 44).

Attach a triangular piece of scrap lumber (called a "pork chop" by some builders) to the siding at the end of the rake fascias.

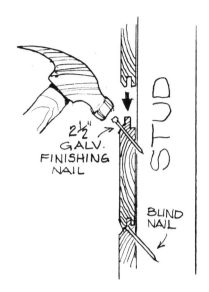

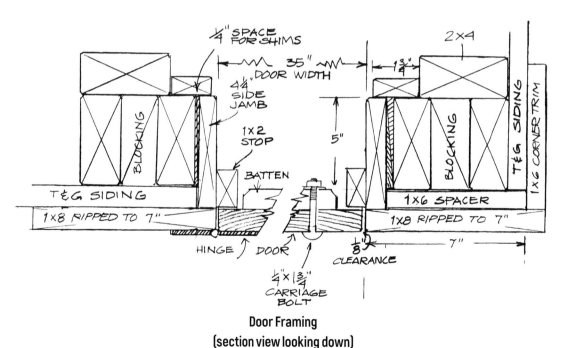

Door Framing
(section view looking down)

Trim Detail

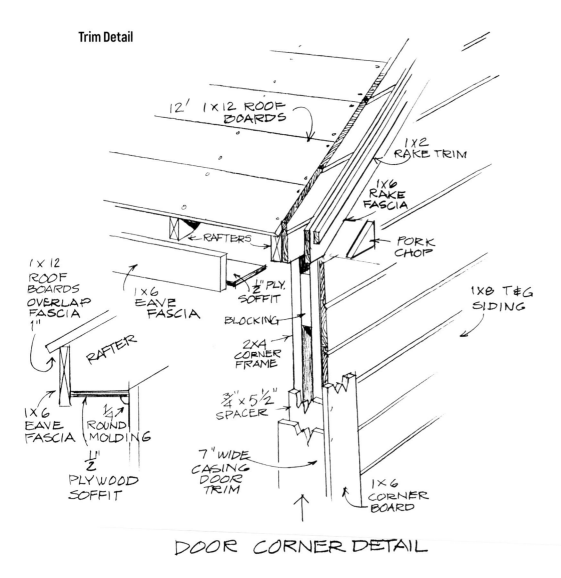

12' 1×12 ROOF BOARDS

1×2 RAKE TRIM

1×6 RAKE FASCIA

RAFTERS

PORK CHOP

1×12 ROOF BOARDS OVERLAP FASCIA 1"

1×6 EAVE FASCIA

RAFTER

½" PLY. SOFFIT

BLOCKING

2×4 CORNER FRAME

1×8 T&G SIDING

1×6 EAVE FASCIA

¼" ROUND MOLDING

½" PLYWOOD SOFFIT

¾" × 5 ½" SPACER

7" WIDE CASING DOOR TRIM

1×6 CORNER BOARD

DOOR CORNER DETAIL

ASPHALT ROOFING

Asphalt shingles are a popular type of roofing in the U.S. because they are long-lasting and comparatively inexpensive.

Begin by stapling the aluminum drip edge to the front and back eaves; staple the rake drip edge to the side edges of the roof. Nail a full 36"-wide strip of 15# asphalt felt (heavy tar paper) over the lower section of the roof so that it overhangs the eave drip edge by ½".

Start the first course of shingles by nailing them upside-down (tabs facing up towards the ridge), overlapping the sides and bottom of the roof by ½". Start the next 3-tab course of shingles on top of the first row with the tabs facing down. This ensures that the rainwater will not seep down through the slots in the shingles. Place ⅜" galvanized shingling nails in each shingle, ⅝" above the tops of the slots. Using tin snips or a utility knife, cut half of one tab from the next row of shingles so that the joints don't line up with the shingles below. Nail another row of shingles (tabs down) to overlap the top of the first row by 4". Continue up the roof in the same manner until you get near the ridge, adding further overlapping strips of asphalt felt as you go; the felt should also overlap the ridge. To make sure your rows are straight, measure from the shingles to the top of the roof, and make adjustments if necessary. At the top of the roof, cut the tabs apart and taper the top portions by ½" (see Ridge Cap Detail on page 46). Fold them over the ridge and overlap them so only the granular part shows.

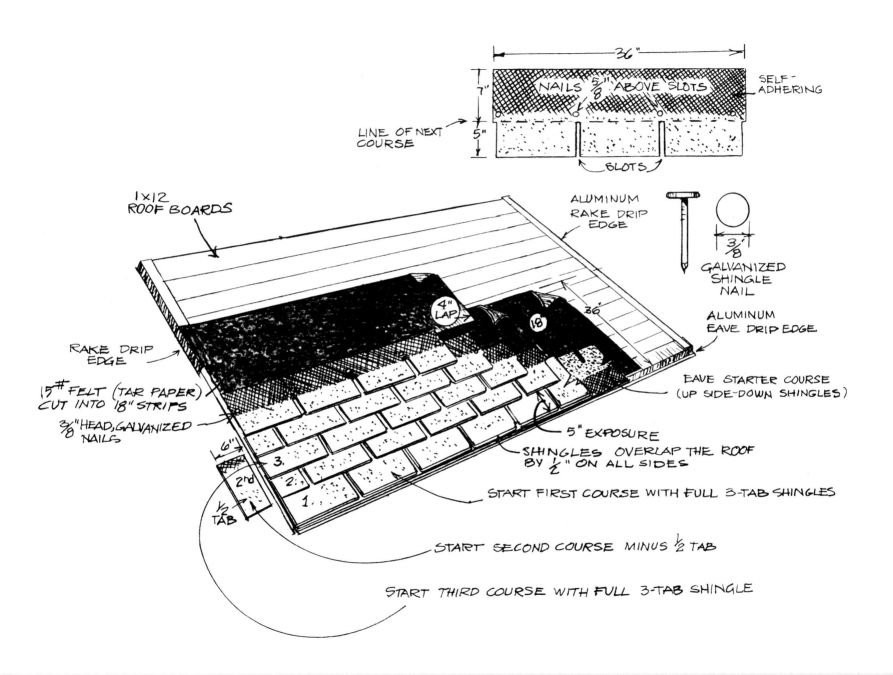

36"

NAILS $\frac{5}{8}$" ABOVE SLOTS

SELF-ADHERING

7"

LINE OF NEXT COURSE

5"

SLOTS

1×12 ROOF BOARDS

ALUMINUM RAKE DRIP EDGE

4" LAP

18

36"

GALVANIZED SHINGLE NAIL

$\frac{3}{8}$"

ALUMINUM EAVE DRIP EDGE

RAKE DRIP EDGE

15# FELT (TAR PAPER) CUT INTO 18" STRIPS

$\frac{3}{8}$" HEAD, GALVANIZED NAILS

6"

3.

2.

1.

2nd

$\frac{1}{2}$ TAB

EAVE STARTER COURSE (UP SIDE-DOWN SHINGLES)

5" EXPOSURE

SHINGLES OVERLAP THE ROOF BY $\frac{1}{2}$" ON ALL SIDES

START FIRST COURSE WITH FULL 3-TAB SHINGLES

START SECOND COURSE MINUS $\frac{1}{2}$ TAB

START THIRD COURSE WITH FULL 3-TAB SHINGLE

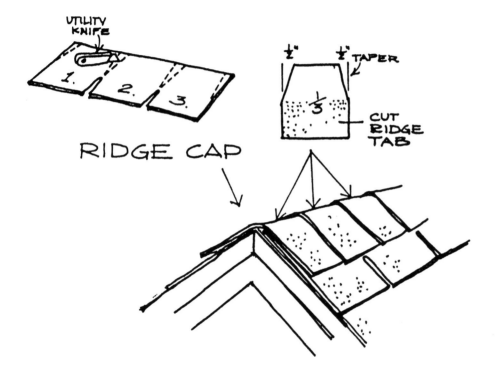

UTILITY KNIFE

1. 2. 3.

RIDGE CAP

½"   ½" TAPER

3

CUT RIDGE TAB

WINDOWS

This cottage also features eco-friendly windows, made from recycled plastic milk bottles. They have the correct muntin profiles and even a slight wood-grain texture. To top it off, they far outlast wooden windows, never need painting and are inexpensive. Unlike pre-hung factory-bought windows that plug into the rough openings, these "barn sashes" do require a little more time to install. This unique window design is adjustable and allows air in while keeping rain out. The windows can easily be lifted out for cleaning and can be replaced with an insect screen in summer.

See General Building Information covering windows and screens, pages 19-21.

LOFT WINDOW

The small window in the loft is optional, but not difficult to make. If you have a table saw it can be done in less than half an hour. *See General Building Information on loft windows, page 20.*

DOOR

Traditionally, shed doors always swing out because this saves valuable storage space inside. There is no raised saddle to sweep over and the wind tends to push the door closed, eliminating drafts. Plus, the building is easier to exit.

The only drawback is that the wind can catch the open door and slam it shut. This can easily be solved by attaching a hook and eye to the door and the building.

As shown on page 47, the rough opening for the door is 37". This allows for ¾" doorjambs on each side, plus ¼" wiggle room for adjusting with shims. Using a table saw, rip-cut two 6' 1x6 boards to 4¼" for the side jambs and another 37" long for the head jamb. Using a handsaw, cut out the 2x4 sole plate between the door studs. Screw the jambs together and set them into the door opening. Use a level to ensure that the door opening is plumb and level, and insert wood shims into the ¼" gap between the jambs and the side studs. Be careful not to force the jambs out of plumb. Screw through the jamb and the shims into the side studs.

Cut five 1x8 tongue and groove boards 74" long (making them 2" longer than the door opening). This will allow the rain to drip off the door and fall away from the front of the shed.

Cut the groove off the first board, and the tongue off the last, so that the five boards together make a door 35" wide. Cut three cross-battens to hold the vertical boards together. These should be 1" shorter on each side than the width of the door (to clear the doorstops). For a more professional appearance, bevel the edges of the battens.

If you plan on using your cabin year-round, you may want to use cross-battens over the entire surface of the door to make it 1½" thick throughout.

Attach the battens to the back of the door using ¼" x 1¾" galvanized carriage bolts.

Cut ¾" x 1½" doorstops from scrap lumber and nail them to the doorjambs.

Cut a 1x2, 35" long, sill strip to fill the space behind the bottom of the door and nail it to the floor frame, flush with the existing floor.

Install 1x6 casing (trim) to the top (head) and sides of the door, overlapping the edge of the jambs by ⅜".

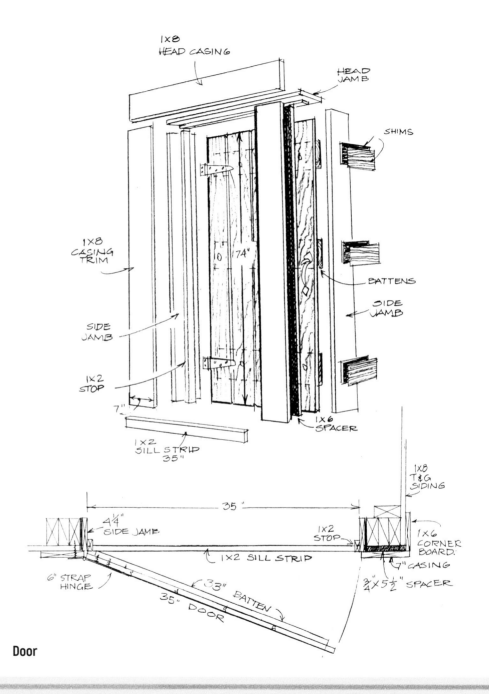

Door

Shim the door up and screw the two strap hinges to the left casing trim. Use extra-long screws at the top to keep the door from sagging. Install the door latch and handle, following the instructions on the package.

SHUTTERS

These shutters are purely decorative to enhance your windows. They are made from the same 1x8 tongue and groove pine boards as the siding. Each shutter is 29" high by two boards wide, joined by two cross-battens. The tongues and grooves are sawn off and the edges of the cross-battens are beveled at 45° to give it a neat appearance.

To attach the cross-battens to the shutterboards, use the same type of carriage bolts that you used on the door. The shutters can be screwed permanently to the structure, using 3" cabinet hangers. Feature the shutters by painting them a special color.

LOFT

A loft is ideal for storage or even to sleep in – plus, it's easy to build. All you need are two 4x4s 10' long, one 2x4 10' long, and four 1x12 shiplap pine boards 12' long.

Space the 4x4s on top of the wall plates at 24" centers and the 10' 2x4 on top of the plates on the end wall. Secure them in place with screws. Cut the 1x12s into 4' lengths, and nail them in place.

SCREENS

You may prefer to replace your windows with screens in the summer to keep uninvited mosquitoes out. These windows can be easily lifted out and replaced with screens. *See General Information – Screens on page 21.*

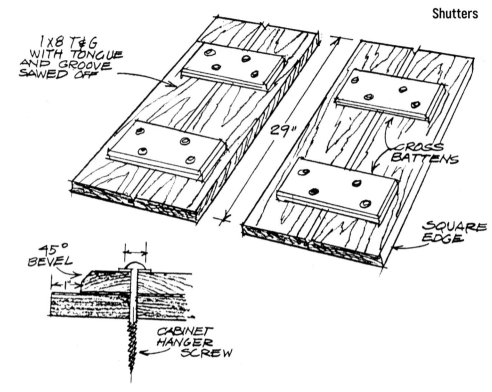

LADDER

The ladder uses four 9' stringers of 1x4 pine and an 8' length of 5/4x4 for the treads. Lean the 1x4s up against the loft, mark a horizontal line at the bottom of the boards, and cut them off at that angle. Using the same angle (approximately 70°), cut 14 pieces of 1x4 (cleats) 13" long. Starting at the bottom, glue and nail the cleats and treads to the 1x4 stringers. Cut a notch out of the back edge of the stringers to rest the ladder on

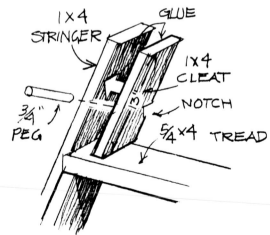

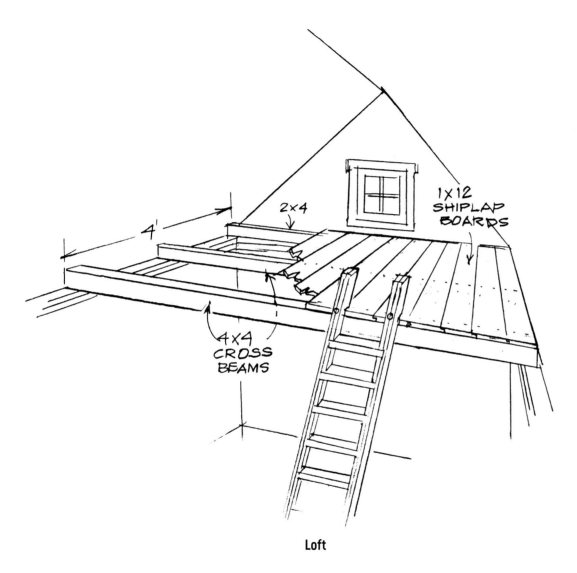

2x4

4'

1X12 SHIPLAP BOARDS

4X4 CROSS BEAMS

Loft

the loft joist. For extra security, drill a hole through the stringers into the loft edge, and insert a wooden peg through each stringer into the joist.

SKYLIGHTS (OPTIONAL)

This tiny house benefits greatly by adding a skylight. You can make one yourself fairly easily and for very little cost. *See General Building Information – Skylights on page 22.*

INTERIORS

There are no limits to the variations on this design.

If you are looking to really go green there are some additional features you can add. Features of the off-grid house include two 80-watt solar panels, a portable wood-burning stove, a catchment system for rain water and fold-out furniture to maximize living space.

For more information, see Section III, Finishing the Interior on page 126.

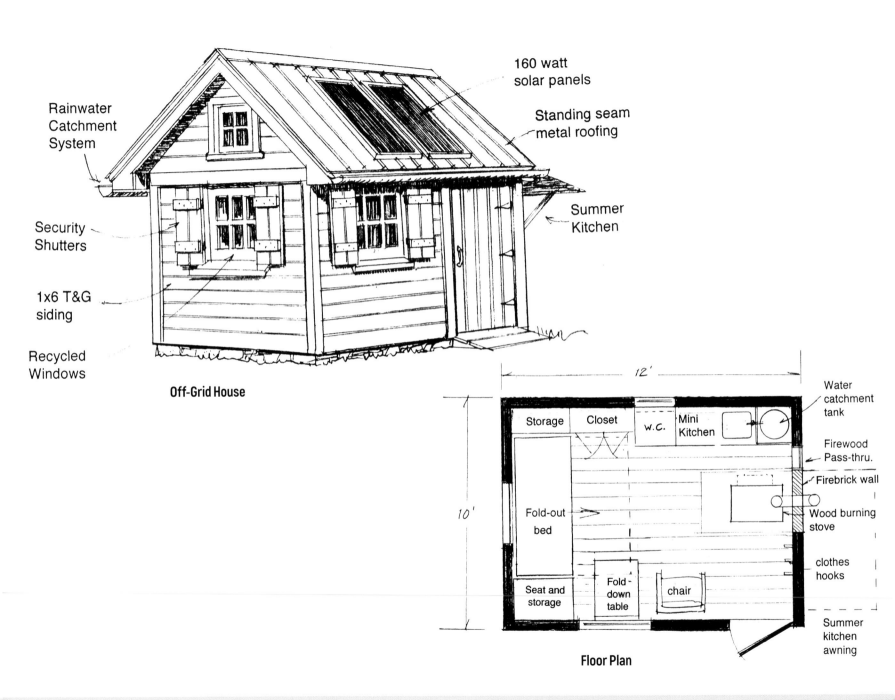

Rainwater
Catchment
System

160 watt
solar panels

Standing seam
metal roofing

Security
Shutters

Summer
Kitchen

1x6 T&G
siding

Recycled
Windows

Off-Grid House

12'

Storage | Closet | w.c. | Mini Kitchen

Water
catchment
tank

Firewood
Pass-thru.

Firebrick wall

Wood burning
stove

10'

Fold-out
bed

clothes
hooks

Seat and
storage

Fold-down table

chair

Summer
kitchen
awning

Floor Plan

tudor backyard cottage

This 8'x11' cottage uses standard 2x4 construction framing; being less than 100 square feet, it will fit on a flat bed truck if you should ever need to move it. The small size also makes it inexpensive to build and easy to heat. We have designed it to make the most efficient use of materials so there is minimal waste. The roof is constructed from five sheets of ¾" plywood, allowing for a slight overhang of the 11' wide house.

This simple structure is suitable for use as a workshop, studio, garden shed, writer's retreat or exercise/yoga/meditation space. The building can be finished in a variety of styles, ranging from rustic Tudor to sleek contemporary. It can easily be increased in size to suit your requirements.

Local conditions will affect your choice of siding material. In more extreme climates, you may want to use insulation, shingles, clapboard or shiplap.

We have clarified and simplified the whole process for the do-it-yourself builder. The information here is presented in both words and pictures in order to be as clear as possible.

THE GOLDEN RECTANGLE

The design of the house is based on The Golden Ratio, which goes by various names, including The Golden Number, Golden Mean, Golden Section and The Divine Proportion. The sides of a Golden Rectangle

are in the Golden Ratio, which is approximately 1 to 1.618. In nature, this ratio is found in structures as diverse as mollusk shells and rose petals; artists from Phidias to Leonardo to Dali have used it – and even today, stretched canvases are sold in the same proportions, echoing the ancient belief in The Golden Ratio's mystical aesthetic appeal.

When designing this building, we superimposed a Golden Rectangle over our plans and were surprised to find it an almost perfect match. It's remarkable to think that our small backyard building follows the same formula that may have shaped The Great Pyramid and The Parthenon. Another happy coincidence is that the base dimensions (10' x 12') are the same numbers that express the pitch (slope) of the roof.

MATERIALS

Qty.	Description	Size	Location
FLOOR			
9	2x8 P.T. wood	8' long	floor joists
2	2x8 P.T. wood	12' long	floor headers
14	2x8 joist hangers		
3	¾" 4x8 ft. AC plywood		floor
WALLS			
7	2x4 #2 pine	12' long	plates & window framing
6	2x4 #2 pine	8' long	end plates
17	2x4 #2 pine	14' long	wall studs (cut in half)
2	2x4 #2 pine	14' long	gable studs
2	2x4 #2 pine	8' long	loft support beams
5	⅝" 4'x8' AC plywood		wall ends including gables
5	⅝" 4'x8' AC plywood		front & back walls
ROOF			
7	2x6 #2 pine	12' long	rafters (cut in half)
1	1x6 #2 pine	12' long	ridge board
2	1x4 #2 pine	12' long	fascia front & back
2	1x6 #2 pine	12' long	fascia gables
20	1x4 #2 pine	12' long	nailers
1	36" roll of 30# asphalt felt		underlayment
10	Bundles, 24" long cedar shakes		
15	Lbs. 6d galvanized nails		
1	1x4 #2 pine	12' long	ledge board
1	1x4 #2 pine	8' long	spacers
2	1x4 #2 cedar	12' long	ridge caps
1	Pair metal scaffolding brackets		
1	2" x 9" scaffolding board (staging plank)	13' long	

FOUNDATIONS

Very few building sites are perfectly flat. One simple solution, used by Frank Lloyd Wright, is to level the ground with stones and then dig a gravel-filled trench, 16" deep and 24" wide, around the perimeter of the structure to drain any water away and avoid potential frost heaving. If your building site slopes away from the structure, consider adding a "drain to daylight" to the bottom of the trench. Another advantage of this foundation is that it allows the building to be moved if necessary, classifying it a "temporary" structure.

Another solution to keep your structure temporary and easily movable is to rest it on concrete blocks, leveled and placed under each corner. Concrete blocks are either 4" or 8" thick and cost about three or four dollars each. If the ground slopes, place more blocks on the lower ground and adjust as necessary. *Also see Foundations on page 17.*

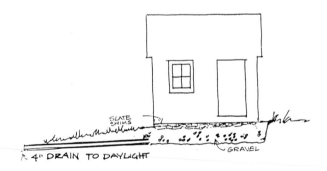

SLATE SHIMS

4" DRAIN TO DAYLIGHT

GRAVEL

WINDOWS			
3	31"x 29" barn sashes (see Sources)		
DOOR			
	30 ft. 1x8 #2 cedar		
	20 ft. 1x6 #2 cedar		
	20 ft. 5/4 x 6 pressure-treated lumber		door trim
	⅛" thick clear acrylic	24" x 24"	door window
HARDWARE			
2	gallons exterior latex, matte white paint with textured additive		
3	cartridges PL 400 construction adhesive		
5	lbs. 6d (2") galvanized common nails		floor & roof
3	lbs., 3" epoxy-coated screws		floor & wall framing
	Hinges		handles & catches (see plans - front elevation)

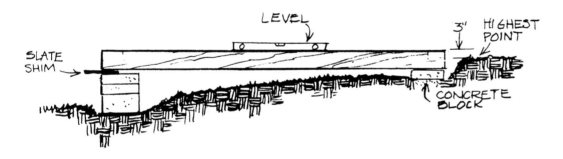

If possible, place the door at the highest point.

FRAMING

Cut the two floor headers (the long sides of the frame) to measure 11'. Cut the nine remaining floor joists to 7' 9". Join the four outside corner boards together using 10d nails (3 per joint); check the corner angles with a roofing square, and use a tape measure to ensure that the diagonals are equal. Measure and mark from each end of the headers 16", 32", 48" and 66". Install the joist hangers at these centers. Seat the joists in the hangers. Nail through the headers into the ends of the joists. Lay a 4x8 sheet of ¾" AC plywood across the frame, flush with one end, and nail in place, approximately every 8" along each joist. Do the same at the other end of the frame, attaching the second sheet of plywood. Trim the third sheet of plywood to 3' x 8' to complete the floor. Build the wall frames on the level platform you have just completed. Make the first long side 11' and prop temporarily in place. Repeat for the second side.

Make the two end walls 7' 5" wide to fit between the long walls. Cut and nail 2x4 horizontal 'cats' (nailers) to fit between the wall studs at a height of 34", to provide a nailing surface for the wall siding. Nail a top plate to the top of the structure, staggering the joints at the corners. Mark the positions of the rafters on the top plate. (See Front Elevation on page 57).

For the roof trusses, cut 20 pieces, 6' long. Cut out the bird's mouth and top plumb cut, (see Rafter Detail on page 59.) Place two rafters on the floor and place a spare 2x4, 8' long, inside the bird's mouth of both rafters. This 2x4 acts as a base to establish the width of the roof truss. From a piece of ¾" thick

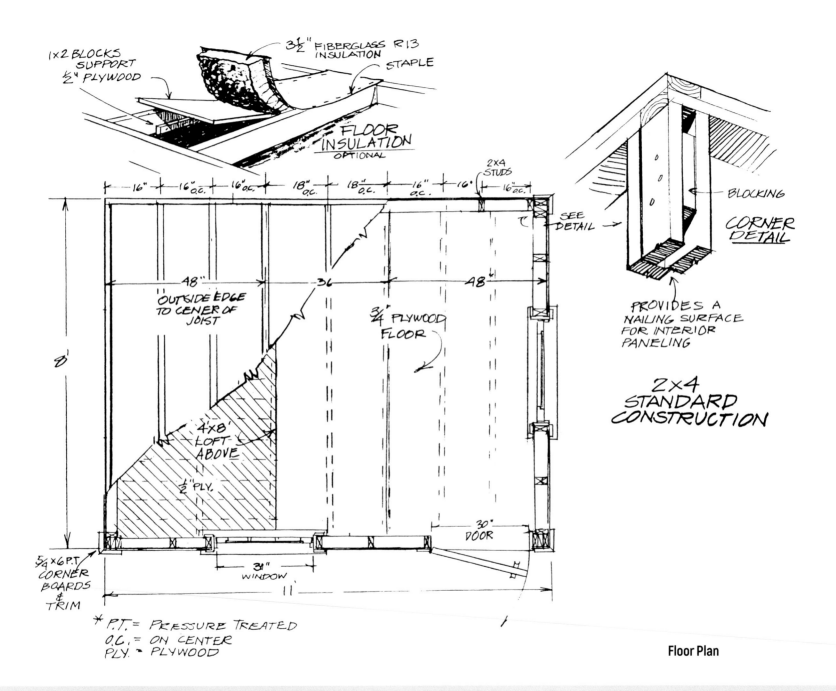

1x2 BLOCKS SUPPORT ½" PLYWOOD

3½" FIBERGLASS R13 INSULATION

STAPLE

FLOOR INSULATION
OPTIONAL

2x4 STUDS

16" | 16" O.C. | 16" O.C. | 18" O.C. | 18" O.C. | 16" O.C. | 16" | 16" O.C.

SEE DETAIL

BLOCKING

CORNER DETAIL

PROVIDES A NAILING SURFACE FOR INTERIOR PANELING

2x4 STANDARD CONSTRUCTION

48"
OUTSIDE EDGE TO CENTER OF JOIST

36"

48"

¾" PLYWOOD FLOOR

8'

4'x8' LOFT ABOVE

½" PLY.

30" DOOR

5/4 x 6 P.T. CORNER BOARDS & TRIM

31" WINDOW

11'

*P.T. = PRESSURE TREATED
O.C. = ON CENTER
PLY. = PLYWOOD

Floor Plan

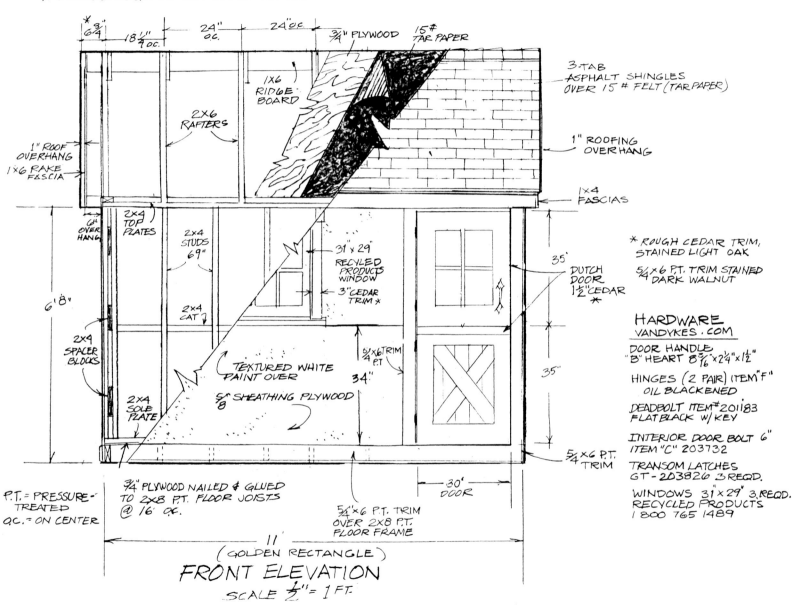

* OUTSIDE EDGE TO CENTER OF RAFTER

24" O.C.

24" O.C.

3/4" PLYWOOD

15# TAR PAPER

* 6 3/4"

18 1/4" O.C.

3-TAB ASPHALT SHINGLES OVER 15# FELT (TAR PAPER)

1X6 RIDGE BOARD

2X6 RAFTERS

1" ROOF OVERHANG

1X6 RAKE FASCIA

1" ROOFING OVERHANG

1X4 FASCIAS

2X4 TOP PLATES

6" OVER HANG

2X4 STUDS 69"

* ROUGH CEDAR TRIM, STAINED LIGHT OAK

5/4 X 6 P.T. TRIM STAINED DARK WALNUT

31" X 29" RECYCLED PRODUCTS WINDOW

3" CEDAR TRIM *

35'

DUTCH DOOR 1 1/2" CEDAR *

6'8"

2X4 CAT

HARDWARE VANDYKES.COM

DOOR HANDLE "B" HEART 8 3/16" X 2 1/4" X 1/2"

2X4 SPACER BLOCKS

TEXTURED WHITE PAINT OVER

5/4 X 6 TRIM P.T

34"

35'

HINGES (2 PAIR) ITEM "F" OIL BLACKENED

DEADBOLT ITEM # 201183 FLATBLACK W/ KEY

2X4 SOLE PLATE

5/8" SHEATHING PLYWOOD

INTERIOR DOOR BOLT 6" ITEM "C" 203732

5/4 X 6 P.T. TRIM

TRANSOM LATCHES GT-203826 3 REQD.

P.T. = PRESSURE-TREATED

O.C. = ON CENTER

3/4" PLYWOOD NAILED & GLUED TO 2X8 P.T. FLOOR JOISTS @ 16' O.C.

5/4" X 6 P.T. TRIM OVER 2X8 P.T. FLOOR FRAME

30' DOOR

WINDOWS 31" X 29" 3 REQD. RECYCLED PRODUCTS 1 800 765 1489

11' (GOLDEN RECTANGLE)

FRONT ELEVATION

SCALE 1/2" = 1 FT.

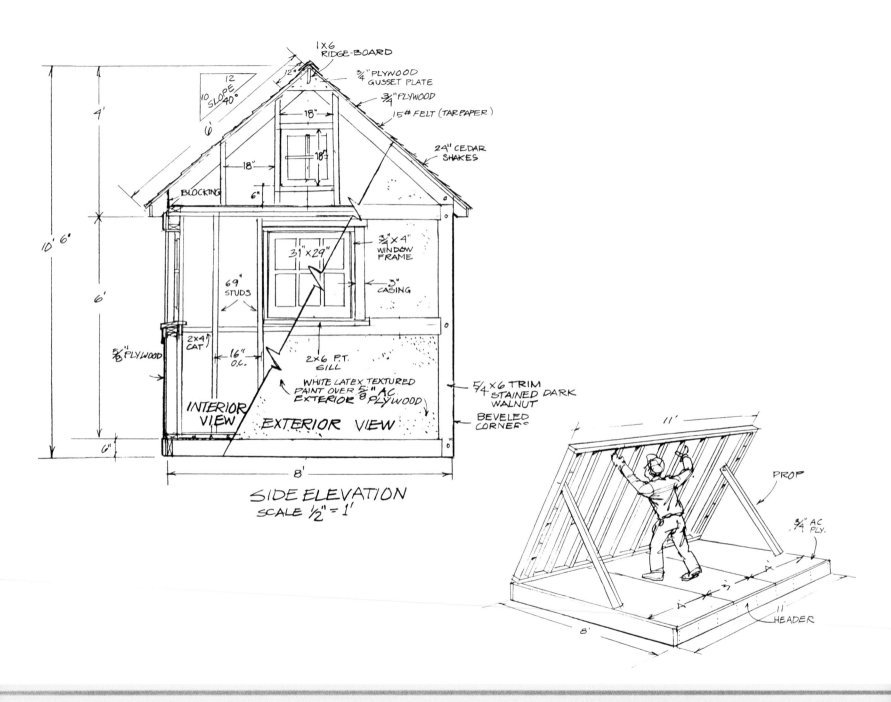

1X6 RIDGE-BOARD

12"

3/4" PLYWOOD GUSSET PLATE

12

10 SLOPE 40°

6'

3/4" PLYWOOD

15# FELT (TAR PAPER)

18"

18"

24" CEDAR SHAKES

BLOCKING

18"

6"

4'

10' 6"

6'

6"

3/4" X 4" WINDOW FRAME

31" X 29"

3" CASING

69" STUDS

2X4" CAT

16" O.C.

5/8" PLYWOOD

2X6 P.T. SILL

WHITE LATEX TEXTURED PAINT OVER 5/8" AC EXTERIOR PLYWOOD

5/4 X6 TRIM STAINED DARK WALNUT

BEVELED CORNERS

INTERIOR VIEW

EXTERIOR VIEW

8'

SIDE ELEVATION
SCALE 1/2" = 1'

11'

PROP

3/4" AC PLY.

3'

4'

8'

11' HEADER

Detail Rafter Template

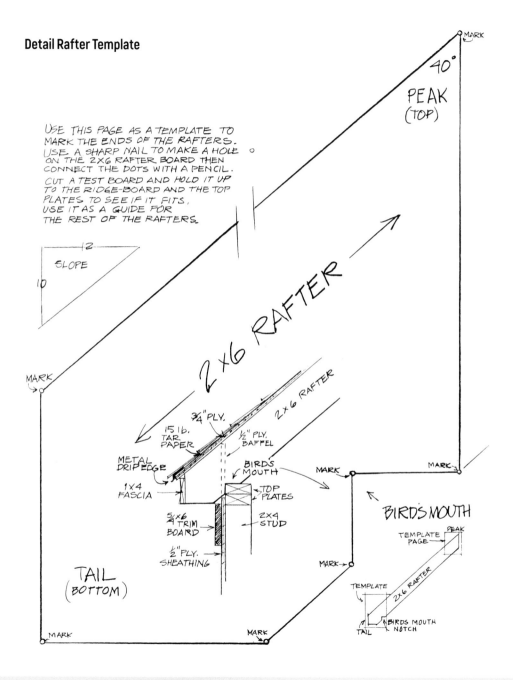

MARK

40°

PEAK
(TOP)

USE THIS PAGE AS A TEMPLATE TO
MARK THE ENDS OF THE RAFTERS.
USE A SHARP NAIL TO MAKE A HOLE
ON THE 2X6 RAFTER BOARD THEN
CONNECT THE DOTS WITH A PENCIL.
CUT A TEST BOARD AND HOLD IT UP
TO THE RIDGE-BOARD AND THE TOP
PLATES TO SEE IF IT FITS,
USE IT AS A GUIDE FOR
THE REST OF THE RAFTERS.

12

SLOPE

10

2×6 RAFTER

MARK

2×6 RAFTER

¾" PLY.

15 lb.
TAR
PAPER

½" PLY.
BAFFEL

METAL
DRIP EDGE

BIRD'S
MOUTH

MARK

MARK

1×4
FASCIA

TOP
PLATES

5/4 ×6
TRIM
BOARD

2×4
STUD

BIRD'S MOUTH

½" PLY.
SHEATHING

MARK

TEMPLATE
PAGE

PEAK

TAIL
(BOTTOM)

TEMPLATE

2×6 RAFTER

MARK

MARK

TAIL

BIRDS MOUTH
NOTCH

plywood, cut nine gusset plates (see Side Elevation, page 58) and screw them to the apex of the rafters. Screw a temporary cross-tie to the rafters, to hold them in place while you raise them. Using a jigsaw, cut out a ¾" x 5½" notch for the ridge board as shown on page 60. Measure and mark the positions of the rafters on the ridge board (See Front Elevation, page 57 and Ridge Board Detail, page 60). Use the ridge board to mark the position of the rafters on the top plate. Screw a 10' temporary mast to the outside center of each end wall to support the end trusses as they are raised. Raise the two end trusses and drop the 1x6 ridge board into the cut-out notches. Lift the remaining roof trusses into position, aligning them with the marks on the top plates and ridge-board. Toenail the roof trusses to the top plates and ridge board.

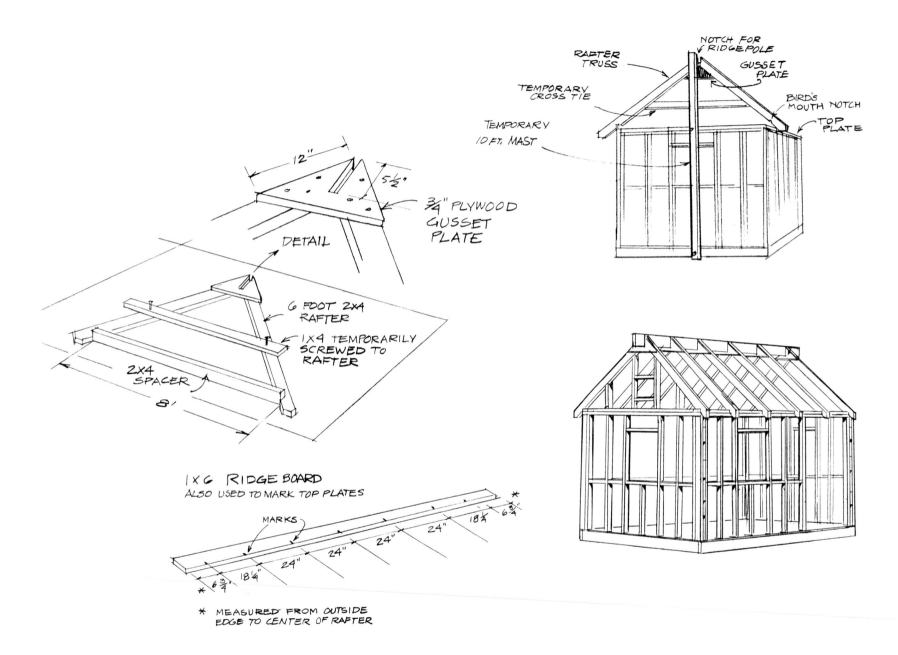

12"

5½"

¾" PLYWOOD
GUSSET
PLATE

DETAIL

6 FOOT 2×4
RAFTER

1×4 TEMPORARILY
SCREWED TO
RAFTER

2×4
SPACER

8'

NOTCH FOR
RIDGEPOLE

RAFTER
TRUSS

GUSSET
PLATE

TEMPORARY
CROSS TIE

BIRD'S
MOUTH NOTCH

TEMPORARY
10 FT. MAST

TOP
PLATE

1×6 RIDGE BOARD
ALSO USED TO MARK TOP PLATES

MARKS

6¾"

18¼"

24"

24"

24"

18¼"

6¾"

* 6¾" 18¼" 24" 24" 24" 18¼" 6¾" *

* MEASURED FROM OUTSIDE
EDGE TO CENTER OF RAFTER

ROOFING WITH CEDAR SHAKES

Nail three 1x4 nailers onto the bottom edge of the rafters. Cut 24 1x4 spacers to 7" lengths. Attach nailers and spacers onto the rafters until you reach the roof ridge. Staple a 36" wide piece of 30# saturated felt onto the bottom nailers, allowing the felt to overhang the bottom edge of the roof by 1".

Nail two layers of cedar shakes to the bottom nailers, overhanging the bottom nailer by 2". The shakes should overhang the side gables by 1¾". Hammer two nails in each shake. Stagger the second layer of shakes so the edges don't line up with the underlying shakes.

Temporarily nail a 1x4 ledge board so its top edge is 10" up from the lower edge of the shakes; this will determine the lower edge of the next course of shakes. Cut a roll of 36" saturated felt in half. Staple an 18" strip to the roof, ½" above the ledge board. Nail the next course of shakes, butting down to the ledge board. Remove the ledge board and reset it so its top edge is 10" above the lower edge of the second course of shakes. Repeat, alternating felt and shakes until you reach the top. Allow the felt to overlap the ridge. As you are working, check that the nails are going through the middle of the nailers. You can see from inside the roof. As you get closer to the top, adjust the rows if necessary so they are parallel with the ridge.

Halfway up the roof, you will need a scaffolding board to stand on. Attach it with metal brackets. Use a hand saw to trim the top course of shakes flush with the ridge.

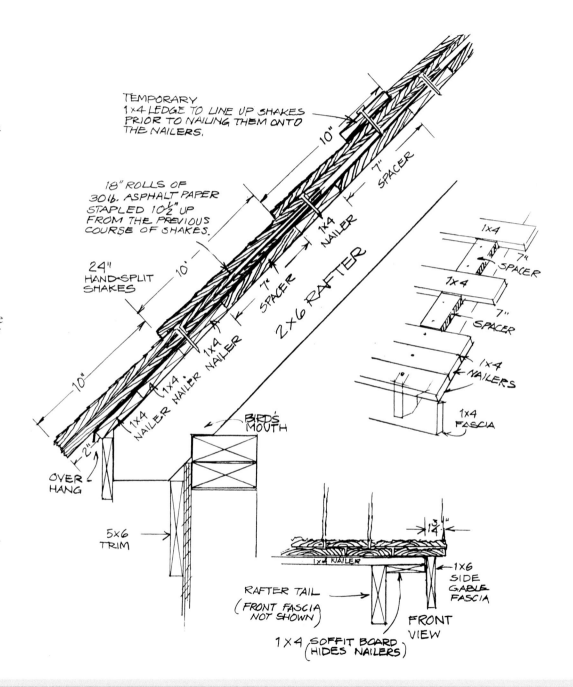

TEMPORARY 1x4 LEDGE TO LINE UP SHAKES PRIOR TO NAILING THEM ONTO THE NAILERS.

18" ROLLS OF 30 lb. ASPHALT PAPER STAPLED 10½" UP FROM THE PREVIOUS COURSE OF SHAKES.

24" HAND-SPLIT SHAKES

2x6 RAFTER

SPACER

7" SPACER

1x4 NAILER

10'

10"

10'

7"

2"

OVER HANG

BIRD'S MOUTH

5x6 TRIM

1x4 NAILER NAILER NAILER

1x4

7" SPACER

1x4

7" SPACER

1x4 NAILERS

1x4 FASCIA

1x4 NAILER

1⅓"

1x6 SIDE GABLE FASCIA

RAFTER TAIL (FRONT FASCIA NOT SHOWN)

1x4 SOFFIT BOARD (HIDES NAILERS)

FRONT VIEW

Follow the same steps with the other side of the roof. Cover the ridge with a 7"-wide piece of saturated felt and nail two pieces of 1x4 rough cedar over the felt.

For an alternate roofing idea, see Asphalt Roofing on page 44.

CLOSING IN

Once the house is framed and the roof is finished, it's time to close it in to the weather. Cut and nail the ⅝" thick sheets of AC plywood to the frame, using 6d galvanized nails. To fill the spaces between the rafter ends (tails), measure, cut and nail pieces of plywood (blocking) to the top plate, caulking any gaps from the inside. Do this before adding the fascia boards. It's a good idea to paint the plywood sheathing now, before attaching the trim. Apply at least two coats of good quality exterior textured paint; follow the manufacturer's directions regarding primers.

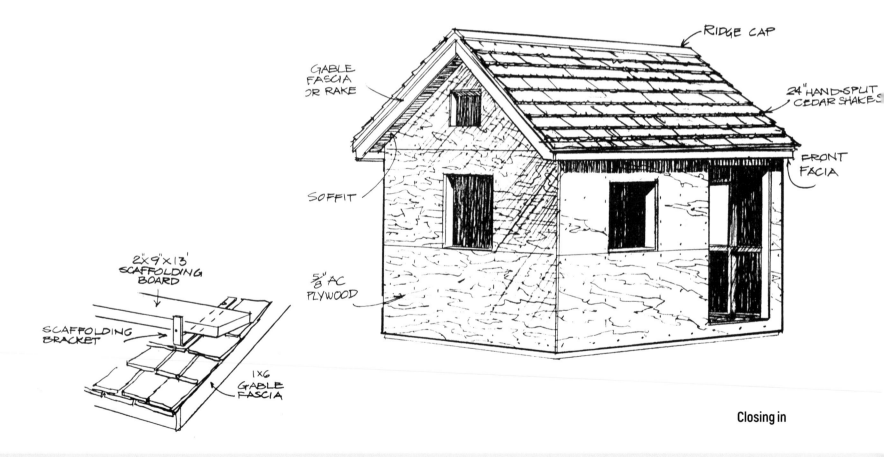

RIDGE CAP

GABLE FASCIA OR RAKE

24" HAND-SPLIT CEDAR SHAKES

FRONT FASCIA

SOFFIT

2"x9"x13' SCAFFOLDING BOARD

SCAFFOLDING BRACKET

⅝" AC PLYWOOD

1x6 GABLE FASCIA

Closing in

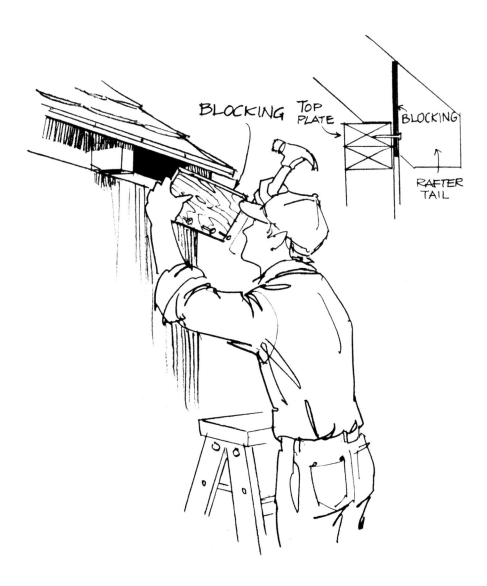

BLOCKING TOP PLATE BLOCKING

RAFTER TAIL

Blocking

DOORS

You will need to make a custom door, since standard doors are 6' 8" high. Your door can be as simple as a piece of ¾" plywood cut to fit the door opening and attached with two heavy-duty strap hinges. Screw two 1x6 cross battens to the back (inside) of the door to stiffen it and to back up the hinges on the front.

You can make a stronger door by using two layers of ¾" boards. The illustration on page 64 shows how to make a Dutch door using the same principle. The upper half of the door has a window made out of Plexiglas set in from the back, using narrow, beveled strips to hold it in place. The ¾" x ⅝" crossed muntins are set into the stiles and rails of the window by ⅜". The oak slide bolt that holds the door shut is a typical feature in many historical buildings and can be made in half an hour - however, if you are worried about security, fit a modern lock.

We recommend that the door hinge outwards because:

- It's easy to sweep over the sill since there is no raised saddle.
- It allows maximum use of interior space.
- It is more draft- and rain-resistant, since the wind will tend to push the door closed rather than open.

When installing the door frame, make sure the hinged side (jamb) is perfectly plumb (vertical), adjusting with shims as necessary.

Make sure the barrel of the hinge extends past the face of the side trim and use extra-long screws on the top hinge so they penetrate the doorjambs.

WINDOWS

Don't underestimate the importance of having enough windows. Windows bring the outdoors inside and there is no substitute for natural light and ventilation.

Buy your windows before you begin framing, to ensure that they will fit. This is especially true if you are using salvaged windows. You can buy factory made pre-hung windows from your local lumberyard and insert them into the rough openings as specified in the manufacture's literature. Popular types of windows are double hung, awning and casement which all come with insulated glass and screens. Although pre-hung windows are easier to install, they are the most expensive. A good alternative is to make your own windows (if you have a table saw) for about $15.

The most economical and eco-friendly windows that you can buy are made from recycled milk bottles (*see Resources, page 201*). They look exactly like traditional windows and can outlast a wood window.

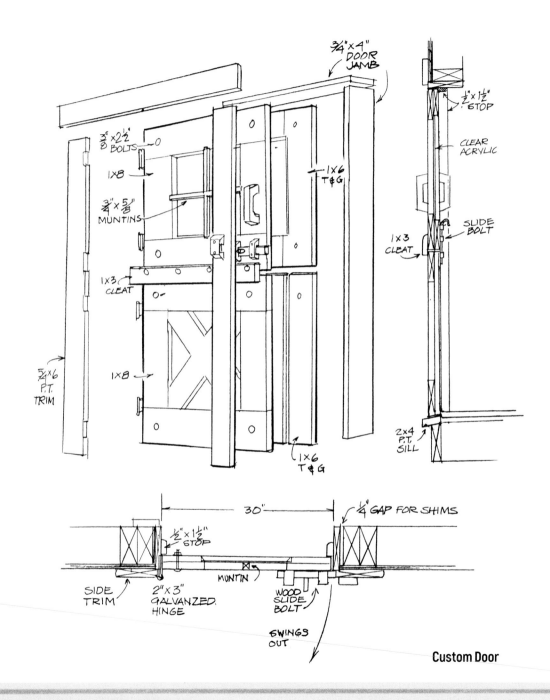

Custom Door

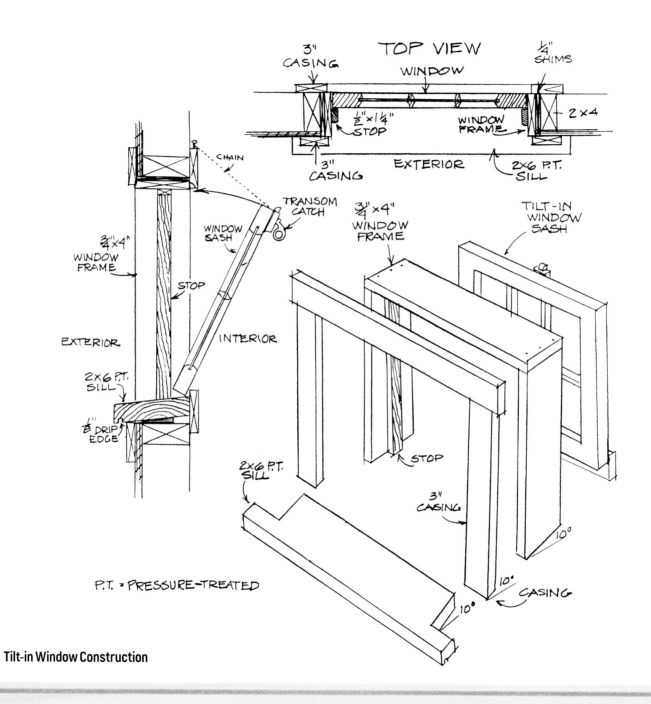

TOP VIEW

3" CASING

WINDOW

¼" SHIMS

½"×1¼" STOP

WINDOW FRAME

2×4

3" CASING

EXTERIOR

2×6 P.T. SILL

CHAIN

TRANSOM CATCH

WINDOW SASH

¾"×4" WINDOW FRAME

STOP

EXTERIOR

INTERIOR

2×6 P.T. SILL

⅛" DRIP EDGE

¾"×4" WINDOW FRAME

TILT-IN WINDOW SASH

STOP

2×6 P.T. SILL

3" CASING

10°

10°

10°

CASING

P.T. = PRESSURE-TREATED

Tilt-in Window Construction

Our favorite way of hanging a single sash window is to mount it so that it tilts inwards at the top. This way the rain won't get in even if the window is open. You can adjust the window opening by attaching a small chain to the transom latch and the top window frame. If you are worried about bugs, you can easily lift it out and attach a homemade screen. Make a window frame out of 1x4s and cut a sill out of 2x6 pressure treated lumber, sloped at 10° to deflect rain. *For detailed instructions & alternative types of windows, see General Building Information pages 19-21.*

INSTALLING THE TRIM

To give your building a timber-framed "Tudor" appearance, buy 1x12 northern pine boards (which are rough on one side) and rip cut them in half so they measure approximately 5¼" wide. Rip several of the boards in half again for the window trim, which should be approximately 2½" wide.

This rough-sawn lumber is perfect for the rustic style of the building, and it's also one of the least expensive types of lumber. If your lumberyard doesn't carry it, try a local sawmill.

Prime the backs and ends of the boards with a sealant. Before nailing up the trim, roughen the edges with a rasp or #24-grit sandpaper on a disk grinder to give the trim a hand-hewn look. This is a little more work but well worth it. Roughen the joints of the

corner boards in the same way, to make them look like 6x6 timbers.

Attach the corner boards using Titebond III exterior glue and 2¼" finishing nails. Install the horizontal and diagonal trim boards in the same way. Caulk all the joints with Phenoseal to prevent rainwater from seeping between the boards and the plywood sheathing.

When making the window trim, cut the bottoms of the vertical pieces (jambs) to the same 10° angle as the pressure-treated sills. Offset the trim ¼" from the inside edge of the window frame and extend the top header trim by ½" on each side to give it a more traditional look.

Cover the underneath of the gable (soffit) to hide the roofing nailers with a board cut to the exact width.

To finish the trim, we used a mixture of 2 parts Minwax Special Walnut Stain to 1 part Golden Oak and 1 part paint thinner. This will penetrate and seal the rough wood, giving it a rustic look without making it too glossy. We find that modern stain sealers can give the wood a phony, waxy look. Before staining the trim, test the color on a scrap piece of the same wood.

You can change the windows and the siding material to give the building a more contemporary look as shown on page 68.

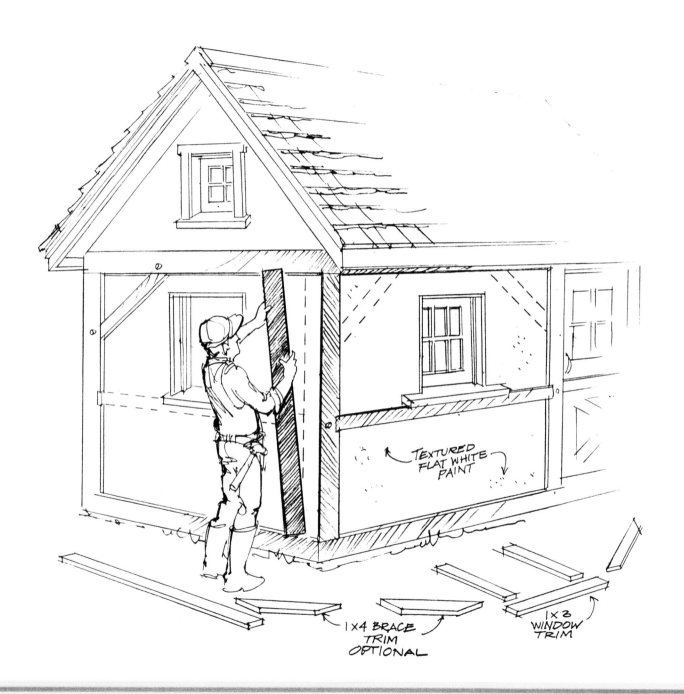

TEXTURED
FLAT WHITE
PAINT

1x4 BRACE
TRIM
OPTIONAL

1x3
WINDOW
TRIM

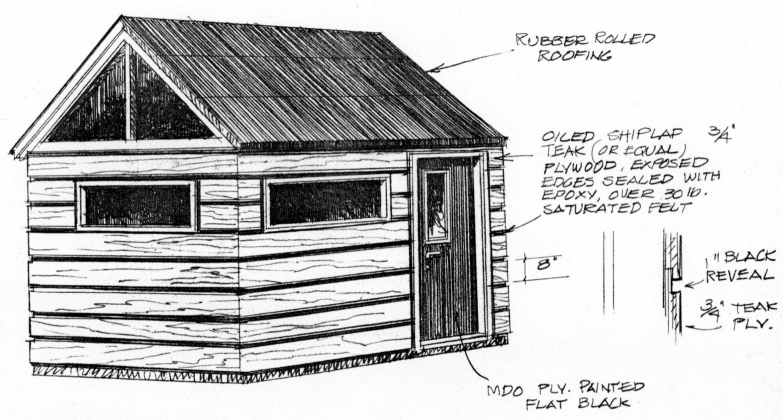

RUBBER ROLLED ROOFING

OILED SHIPLAP 3/4"
TEAK (OR EQUAL)
PLYWOOD, EXPOSED
EDGES SEALED WITH
EPOXY, OVER 30 lb.
SATURATED FELT

8"

1" BLACK REVEAL

3/4" TEAK PLY.

MDO PLY. PAINTED FLAT BLACK

CTR 4010 ANDERSON CASEMENT WINDOWS

Contemporary Backyard Cottage

japanese guest house

We originally designed this 200 sq. ft. house as a pool house, but later changed it into a guesthouse for our daughter and her husband when they come to visit. It is big enough for two adults to spend a few nights. There's a small bathroom and a queen-size murphy bed which lifts up to reveal a Japanese-style tea table and four fold-up stools for guests; in the corner is a refrigerator and sink with a triangular counter. A 4' wide deck surrounds the 14' x 14' building, leading to an outdoor shower at the back. The two 8' wide sliding doors face southeast to catch the early morning and noonday sun.

The homeowner/builder should check with the local building department to see what, if any, permits are required.

This tiny house could easily be built by one or two people who have a little construction experience. The design does not require a concrete foundation; instead, the floor rests 18" above ground level, on 6 x 6 pressure-treated posts buried below the frost line. You can set all the posts in a day given the right soil conditions.

The floor frame and deck are made of stock pressure-treated lumber, stained later to match the exterior walls. The floor is ¾" exterior plywood, covered with finished flooring after the building is enclosed.

The walls are standard 2x6 stud framing with boxed headers (see Box Beam detail on page 71) to support the roof. To build the roof, place a 8' x 8' square support box in the center of the building on temporary posts until the rafters are installed.

One of the nice features of this house is the large central skylight, which bathes the interior with light during the day and allows

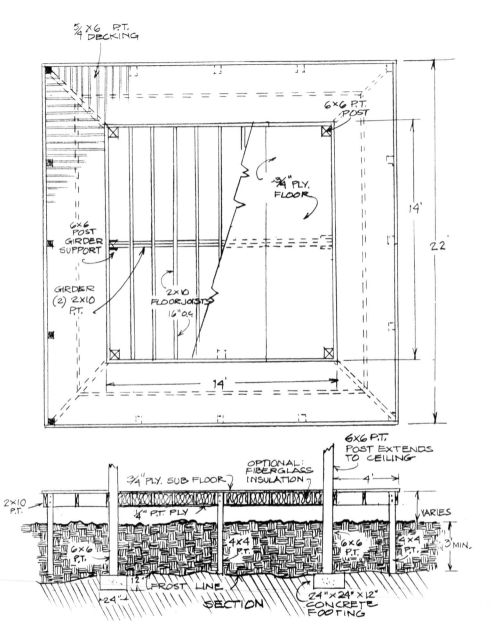

Foundation & Floor Framing

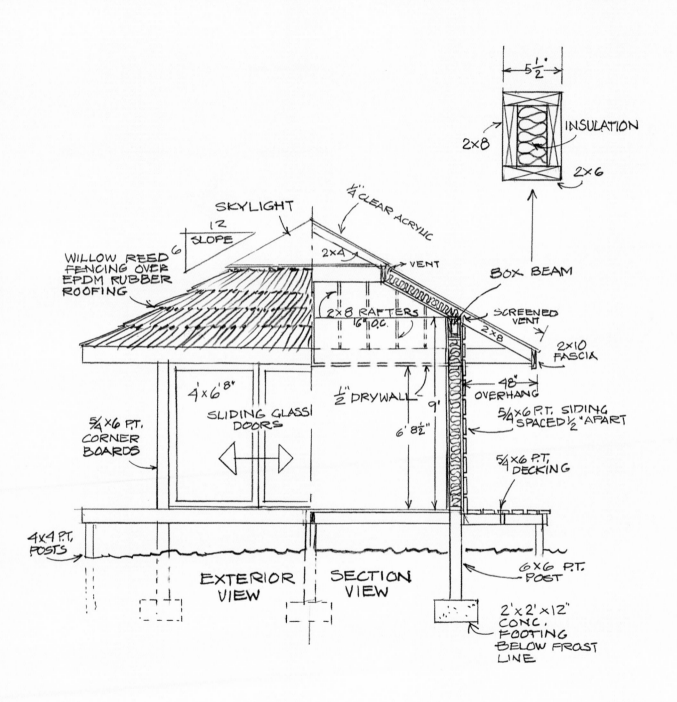

INSULATION

2×8

2×6

5 1/2"

SKYLIGHT

12
6 SLOPE

1/4" CLEAR ACRYLIC

2×4

VENT

BOX BEAM

WILLOW REED FENCING OVER EPDM RUBBER ROOFING

2×8 RAFTERS
16" O.C.

SCREENED VENT

2×8

2×10 FASCIA

48" OVERHANG

4'×6'8"
SLIDING GLASS DOORS

1/2" DRYWALL

9'

6' 8 1/2"

5/4 ×6 P.T. SIDING SPACED 1/2" APART

5/4 ×6 P.T. CORNER BOARDS

5/4 ×6 P.T. DECKING

4×4 P.T. POSTS

EXTERIOR VIEW

SECTION VIEW

6×6 P.T. POST

2'×2'×12" CONC. FOOTING BELOW FROST LINE

you to see the stars at night before you go to sleep. (See Section View, page 71.)

The skylight is made out of four 4' x 8' pieces of ¼" Plexiglas (clear acrylic). Cut the triangular pieces with beveled edges and join together using clear silicone; attach them to a pyramidal framework made of 2x4s painted white.

We first covered the exterior walls with black 30# asphalt paper felt, then sheathed them using 5/4 x 6 pressure-treated horizontal boards spaced ½" apart to give it a contemporary look. To add to the appearance, we painted the sheathing boards and the deck with a coat of Minwax cedar stain, giving the walls the elegant look of teak.

The interior walls are insulated with fiberglass batts and covered with ½" gypsum drywall, painted white.

The sliding glass doors are Andersen *(see Resources, page 201).*

The interior plan and section views show a suggested layout of furniture and appliances:

With a composting toilet (check to see if these are allowed in your area) you may only need a 4' x 4' drywell to drain off the grey water from your shower and sinks. Water can be either collected on the roof or brought from the main house by hose or pipes; hot water can be supplied using an on-demand heater, or a solar or propane water heater *(see Resources).*

This tiny building could be heated by a wood-burning stove on cool nights, but since it's intended to be used mostly during the spring, summer and fall months we recommend electric baseboard heating.

Electricity can be brought in from a sub-panel in the main house through an underground line *(see Wiring, page 134);*

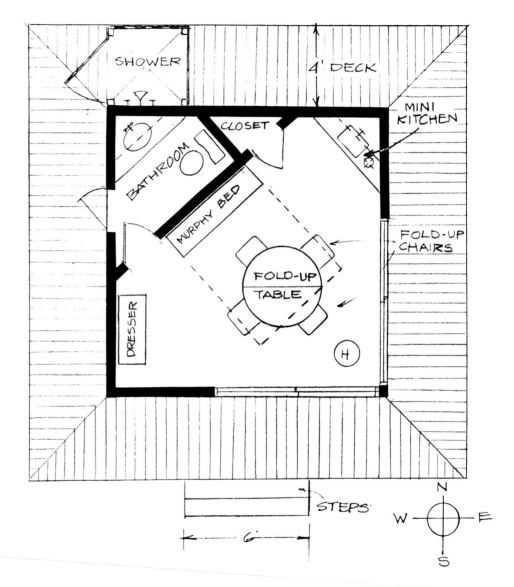

Floor Plan

Diagonal Section View
(corner to corner)

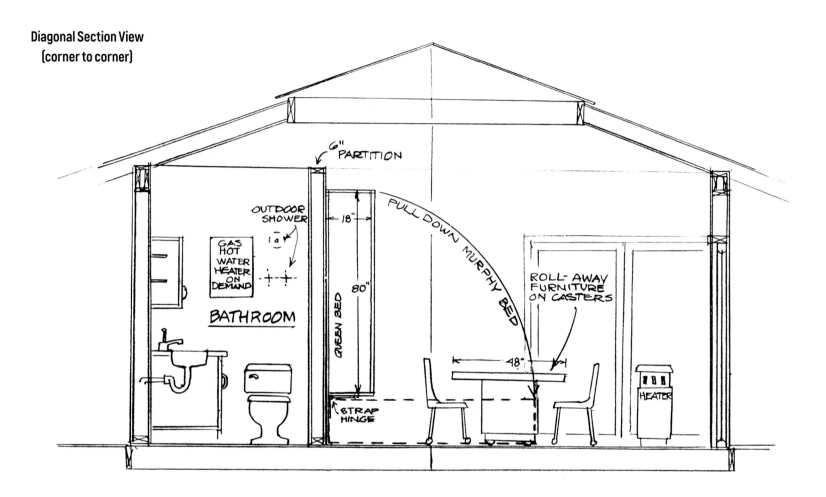

6" PARTITION

OUTDOOR SHOWER

GAS HOT WATER HEATER ON DEMAND

BATHROOM

18"

80"

QUEEN BED

PULL DOWN MURPHY BED

ROLL-AWAY FURNITURE ON CASTERS

48"

STRAP HINGE

HEATER

alternatively, use propane, oil or gas lamps *(see Lighting, page 127)*.

This design has a built-in refrigerator (see refrigerators) in the corner; above the small sink is a corner cabinet for a plastic tank of potable water. If you'd rather not see a kitchen at all, you can have a concealed kitchen *(see Resources: Yestertec Design Company)*.

The bathroom has a door leading out to the deck and outdoor shower. The door is frosted glass, to let in light while maintaining privacy.

The 6/12 sloped pyramidal roof is insulated with R30 fiberglass insulation covered with ¾" exterior plywood, EPDM rubber roofing material, and rolled willow fencing that comes in rolls 3'3" high x 13' wide *(see Resources)*. Cut the willow in half lengthwise and staple it to the plywood.

If money is no object, a Hwam contemporary wood burning stove lends itself well to this modern Japanese-style guest house *(see Resources)*.

weekend retreat on the hudson river

We built this tiny cabin for ourselves; it is just comfortable enough for two – with a bed and table that fold out from the wall (like a sleeper train). Using only hand tools, we worked over the spring, summer and fall on weekends, using our car to carry lumber to the site. We insulated the interior with fiberglass matts, covered with cypress tongue and groove horizontal boards. We sheathed the exterior with ⅝" fir Texture #111 plywood with redwood trim.

This is basically a pole-built structure in which the round poles are replaced by 4x4 square posts, sheathed with 1x4 and pressure-treated southern pine for strength and appearance. We buried the posts 4' into the ground and reinforced them with rocks cemented around the base. The outside corners of the posts mark an area 8' x 12'. We didn't fill in the holes around the posts until the framing was complete, to allow for any adjustments.

Note: We used 14' posts for our cabin, but your site might be more or less steep – measure your site before you order the posts.

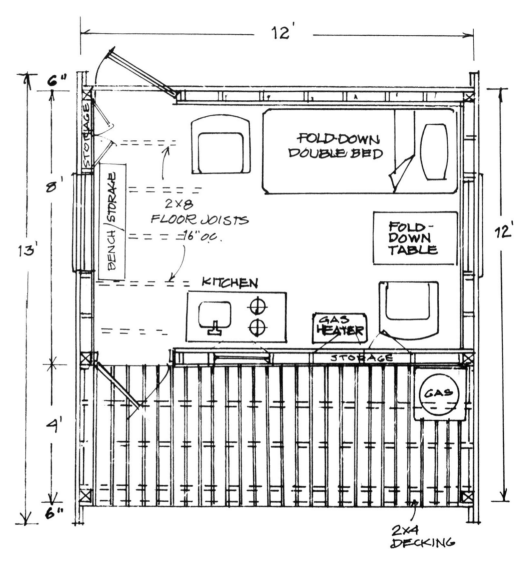

Floor Plan

MATERIALS

These materials are for building the shell of the cabin only. They do not include features such as: interior wall paneling, flooring and furnishings, which will depend on your taste and budget.

Qty.	Description	Size	Location
FRAME			
4	4x4 PT lumber	14'	corner posts
8	1x4 PT lumber	14'	corner post sheathing
8	1x6 PT lumber	14'	corner post sheathing
4	2x10 PT lumber	14'	top side beams
5	2x10 PT lumber	12'	top cross beams
4	2x10 PT lumber	14'	bottom side beams
6	2x10 PT lumber	12'	bottom cross beams
4	4x4 PT lumber	4'	braces
FLOOR			
7	2x8 PT lumber	12'	joists
3	sheets	4'x8' ¾" ext. ply.	flooring
WALLS			
30	2x4 #2 fir	8'	studs
As needed	#2 fir framing for door & window openings	2x4	
9	sheets texture 1-11 ply	4'x8' ⅝"	sheathing
	Insulation	3½"	fiberglass insulation
ROOF			
5	2x8 PT lumber	12'	rafters
4	sheets	4'x8' ¾" ext. ply.	roof deck
3	1x4 PT lumber	12'	edge strips
3	2x4 PT lumber	12'	cant strips
3	1x4 PT lumber	12'	fascia
6	roll aluminum flashing	10' x 6"	roof (& base of walls)
1	roll mineral surfaced rolled roofing	36" wide	

FRAMING

Begin by attaching the lower crossbeams and side beams to the corner posts, using 5" lag screws. Do the same for the top beams, making sure the posts are vertical and the frame is square. Fasten the front crossbeams to the side beams with 4" deck screws. Use lag screws to attach the three rail posts to the lower front crossbeam, and to screw the inner crossbeams to the insides of the corner posts and rail posts. Cut the inner side beams to fit between the crossbeams, and fasten with 2½" deck screws. Before fitting the sections that support the deck, cut notches for the two 2x8 floor joists. Cover the corner posts below the side beams with the 1x4 and 1x6 sheathing (see Post Detail on page 79).

Cut off the ends of the 4x4 corner braces at 45° angles. Attach two of them to the front posts and to the lower front cross beams; use 7" bolts to go all the way through the crossbeams. Drill and counter-sink holes through the bottom corner of each brace and attach to the posts with ½" x 7" lag screws. Hide the heads of the lag screws with wooden plugs, glued into the hole.

The two rear braces face the front of the building and require a 1½" deep shoulder to accommodate the double side beam (see Brace Detail on page 77).

Miter and screw the 2x6 deck railing to the rail posts and corner posts.

Once the framing is finished, it's a good idea to paint it with two coats of stain/sealer. This will avoid accidental drips on the sheathing later. We used a dark brown to blend in with the tree trunks and to contrast with the plywood siding.

DECK & RAILING			
36	2x4 PT lumber	4'	deck boards
3	4x4 PT lumber	42"	posts
2	2x6 PT lumber	4'	side rails
1	2x6 PT lumber	12'	front rail
OTHER MATERIAL			
Doors, windows (See General Information)			
7" bolts, ½ x 5" lag screws, ½ x 7" lag screws, 2½" deck			
screws, galvanized nails			
Cement			
Stain or wood preservative			
Silicone caulk			
Construction adhesive			

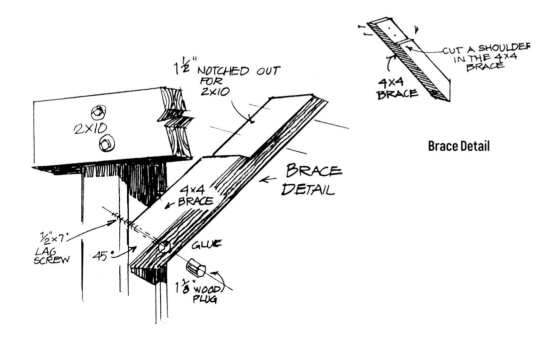

Brace Detail

Using metal joist hangers, nail the five 2x8 floor joists to the 2x10 side beams at 16" centers. Cut the two deck joists to fit the previously cut notches in the side beams. Attach through the side beams, into the joists, using 4" deck screws.

FLOOR
Nail three sheets of exterior plywood to the joists to make the floor. You'll need to notch out the corners of the plywood to fit around the posts. To make the deck, nail 2x4s to the joists.

WALLS
Nail down the sole plates, and frame the walls with 2x4 studs at 16" centers. The front and rear studs are sandwiched between the crossbeams. At the sides you will need to notch out the top of each stud to allow for the double side beams as shown on page 79. Frame the openings for the windows and doors with 2x4s. Attach 6" wide aluminum flashing to the base of the walls, using galvanized nails. Cut and nail the plywood siding to the studs.

ROOF
Frame the roof by installing 2x8 roof joists at 16" centers, using metal joist hangers. Cover it with ¾" plywood, nailed to the ceiling joists and beams. Extend the roof 2" on the front and sides by screwing a 1x4 to the top beams. Make cant strips by beveling an edge of three 2x4s, and attach them to the top of the 1x4s at the sides and front. Omit the strip from the rear of the roof, to allow the rain to run off. Nail a 1x4 fascia board to the edge

of the roof, and stain to match the rest of the trim. Use flashing along the back edge. Lay and glue two layers of rolled roofing to plywood roof.

WINDOWS & DOORS

For information on windows and doors, consult the general building information and "The Versatile Tiny House" instructions: for windows, see pages 19-21; for door information see pages 46-48.

INTERIOR

We insulated the walls with fiberglass batts stapled between the studs; we left out the insulation in a couple of places and used the space to build wall cabinets for kitchen supplies and a first-aid kit.

To give the hut a fresh Scandinavian look, we made the interior walls and ceiling out of 1x6 tongue and groove cypress (laid horizontally), which has a beautiful grain and is impervious to water. We chose a heavy jute floor covering that lasted well and dried quickly if our boots tracked in the snow.

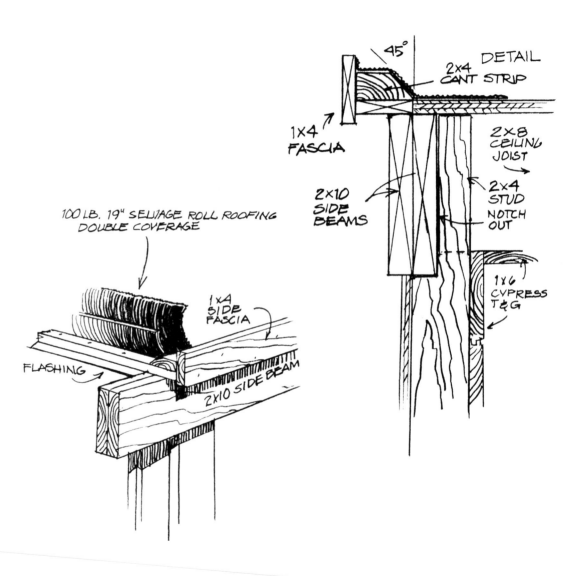

45°

DETAIL

2x4 CANT STRIP

1x4 FASCIA

2x8 CEILING JOIST

2x10 SIDE BEAMS

2x4 STUD NOTCH OUT

1x6 CYPRESS T&G

100 LB. 19" SELVAGE ROLL ROOFING DOUBLE COVERAGE

1x4 SIDE FASCIA

FLASHING

2x10 SIDE BEAM

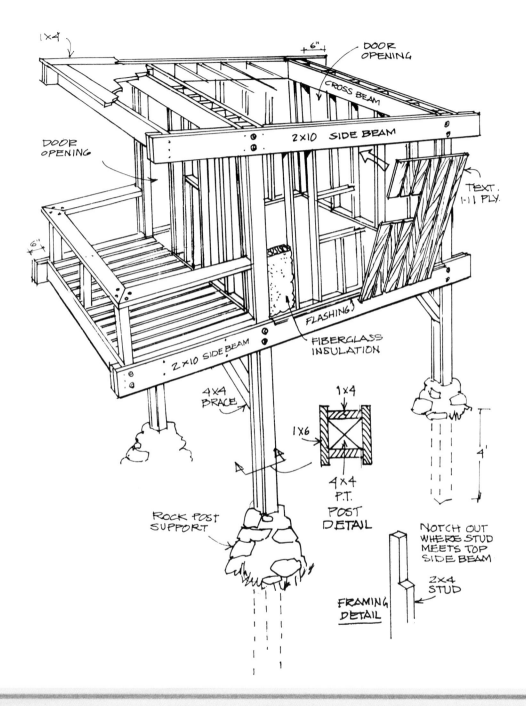

1×4

6"

DOOR OPENING

CROSS BEAM

2×10 SIDE BEAM

DOOR OPENING

TEXT. 1-11 PLY.

6"

FLASHING

FIBERGLASS INSULATION

2×10 SIDE BEAM

4×4 BRACE

4'

ROCK POST SUPPORT

1×4

1×6

4×4 P.T. POST DETAIL

NOTCH OUT WHERE STUD MEETS TOP SIDE BEAM

2×4 STUD

FRAMING DETAIL

moon treehouse

BUILDING SMALL

The Swiss Family Robinson lived in one, Tarzan lived in one, whole tribes have lived in them – including the Korowai people of New Guinea, who built treehouses as high as 140' above the ground on ironwood stilts. Sure treehouses are great for recreation and relaxation, but they can make great living or office spaces as well.

This two-level treehouse was built for a hedge-fund giant who wanted to unwind after a hard day's work on Wall Street, to meditate and practice yoga. He and his wife showed us a picture of their dream: a thatched gazebo with a beautiful view of a remote valley and distant mountains – the ideal setting to contemplate the universe and one's own place in it. They had even picked a site for the treehouse – down steps, past a pool and gardens to a large triple-branched tree silhouetted against the sky but nestled unobtrusively among other trees.

This was not to be some mega-mansion treehouse with high definition television, surround sound, air conditioning and a top-of-the-line refrigerator. It would be a place to get away from the rest of the world, to breathe freely and listen to the soft sound of the bubbling brook below.

With this in mind, we designed a Japanese-style treehouse with a flight of hand-carved stairs leading to an upper deck. Sliding shoji-style pocket doors feature a 4'-diameter translucent circular window. Interior lights are programmed to come on at dusk and project a soft glow visible from the main house. We call it the "Moon Treehouse."

The first step in planning the treehouse was to place long measuring sticks in the

branches of the tree and take photos from several different angles to determine where the main support beams should go. From this information we were able to design the tree-house and submit an accurate rendering of it to our clients. We then made detailed plans for the builder to begin work.

As you can see from the plans, the main trunks of the tree go right through the roof and interior of the house, while the front is supported by two cedar posts (see the Post Detail on page 83). The main girders are bolted to the base of the tree using 1" x 10" stainless steel lag screws, and the floor frame consists of pressure-treated 2x10 floor joists covered with 2" x 9" scaffolding boards. The stairs are made of 3x10 stringers and 4"-diameter peeled cedar poles.

The railings on both top and bottom levels are 4"-diameter peeled cedar poles interwoven with our signature Hempex rope for a rustic look.

We framed the interior using cedar poles and lightweight MDO panels, painted white, to echo traditional Japanese construction. The roof is covered with willow reed fencing material (see the Roof Detail on page 83).

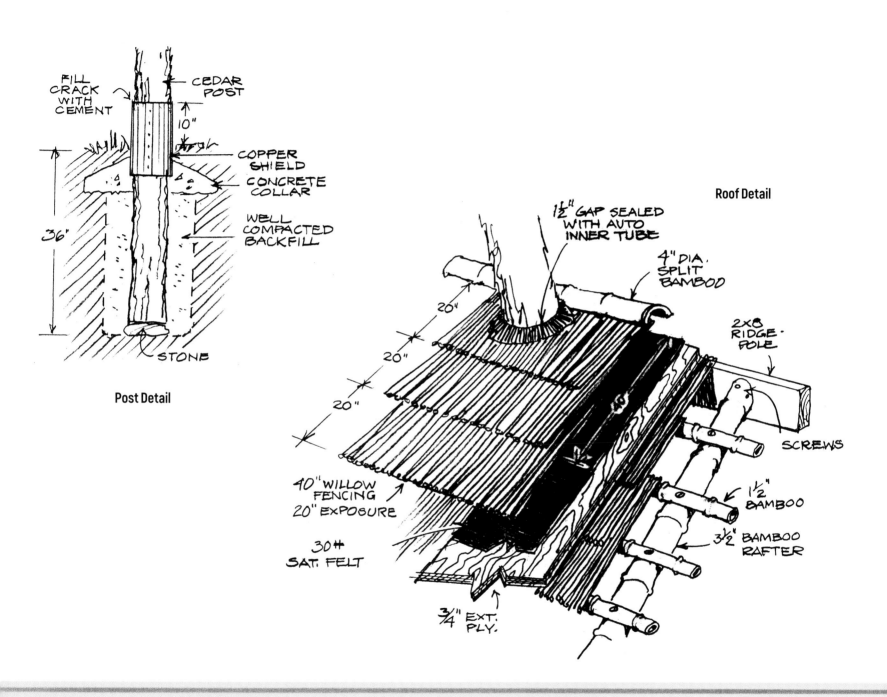

Post Detail

FILL CRACK WITH CEMENT

CEDAR POST

10"

COPPER SHIELD

CONCRETE COLLAR

WELL COMPACTED BACKFILL

36"

STONE

Roof Detail

1½" GAP SEALED WITH AUTO INNER TUBE

4" DIA. SPLIT BAMBOO

2x8 RIDGE-POLE

20"

20"

20"

SCREWS

1½" BAMBOO

3½" BAMBOO RAFTER

40" WILLOW FENCING 20" EXPOSURE

30# SAT. FELT

¾" EXT. PLY.

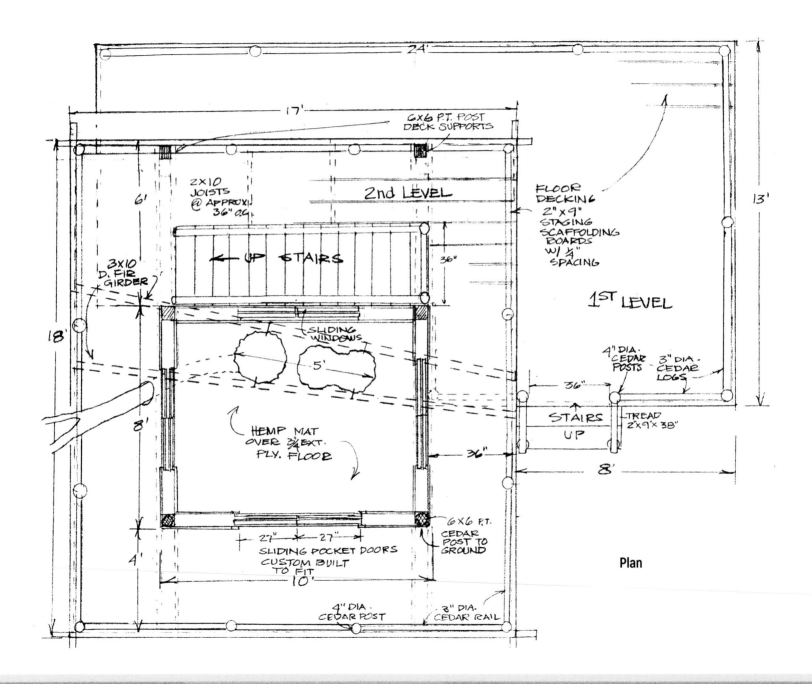

24'

17'

6X6 P.T. POST
DECK SUPPORTS

2X10
JOISTS
@ APPROXI.
36" O.C.

2nd LEVEL

6'

FLOOR
DECKING
2"X9"
STAGING
SCAFFOLDING
BOARDS
W/ ¼"
SPACING

13'

3X10
D. FIR
GIRDER

UP STAIRS

36"

1ST LEVEL

18'

SLIDING
WINDOWS

5'

4" DIA.
CEDAR
POSTS

3" DIA.
CEDAR
LOGS

36"

8'

HEMP MAT
OVER ¾ EXT.
PLY. FLOOR

STAIRS
UP

TREAD
2"x9"x 38"

36"

8'

4'

27"   27"

6X6 P.T.
CEDAR
POST TO
GROUND

Plan

SLIDING POCKET DOORS
CUSTOM BUILT
TO FIT

10'

4" DIA.
CEDAR POST

3" DIA.
CEDAR RAIL

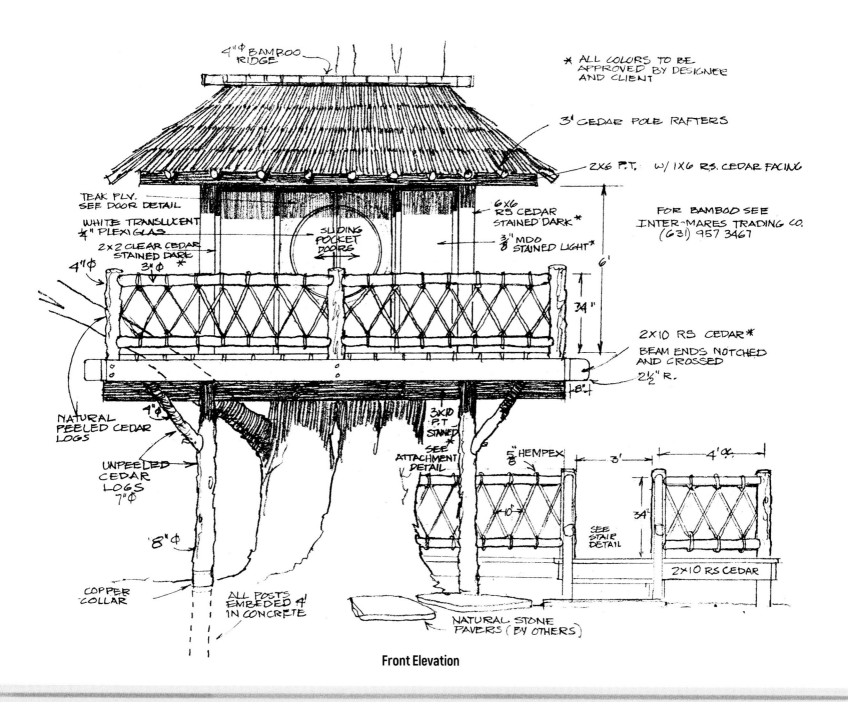

4"Ø BAMBOO RIDGE

* ALL COLORS TO BE APPROVED BY DESIGNEE AND CLIENT

3' CEDAR POLE RAFTERS

2X6 P.T. W/ 1X6 R.S. CEDAR FACING

TEAK PLY. SEE DOOR DETAIL

6X6 RS CEDAR STAINED DARK *

FOR BAMBOO SEE INTER-MARES TRADING CO. (631) 957 3467

WHITE TRANSLUCENT 4" PLEXIGLAS

3/8" MDO STAINED LIGHT *

2X2 CLEAR CEDAR STAINED DARK

SLIDING POCKET DOORS

4"Ø

3"Ø *

6'

34"

2X10 RS CEDAR *

BEAM ENDS NOTCHED AND CROSSED 2½" R.

8"

NATURAL PEELED CEDAR LOGS

4"Ø

3X10 P.T. STAINED * SEE ATTACHMENT DETAIL

5/8" HEMPEX

3'

4'Ø

UNPEELED CEDAR LOGS 7"Ø

10"

SEE STAIR DETAIL

34"

8"Ø

2X10 RS CEDAR

COPPER COLLAR

ALL POSTS EMBEDDED 4' IN CONCRETE

NATURAL STONE PAVERS (BY OTHERS)

Front Elevation

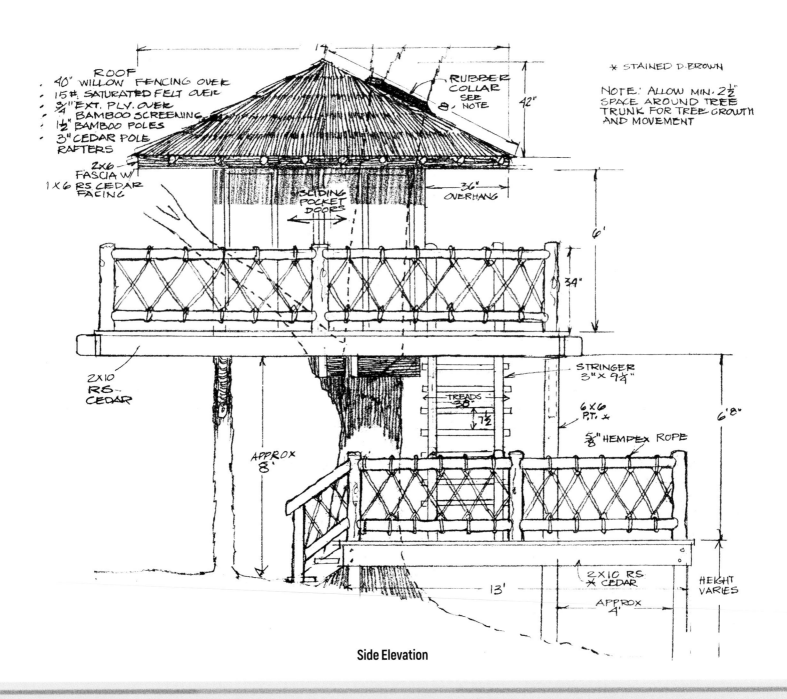

ROOF
- 40" WILLOW FENCING OVER
- 15# SATURATED FELT OVER
- 3/4" EXT. PLY. OVER
- 4" BAMBOO SCREENING
- 1½" BAMBOO POLES
- 3" CEDAR POLE RAFTERS

2x6 FASCIA W/
1x6 RS CEDAR FACING

RUBBER COLLAR SEE NOTE

✳ STAINED D. BROWN

NOTE: ALLOW MIN. 2½" SPACE AROUND TREE TRUNK FOR TREE GROWTH AND MOVEMENT

42"

SLIDING POCKET DOORS

36" OVERHANG

6'

34"

2x10 RS CEDAR

APPROX 8'

STRINGER 3" x 9¼"

6x6 P.T. ✳

⅝" HEMPEX ROPE

TREADS 20"

7½"

6'8"

2x10 RS ✳ CEDAR

HEIGHT VARIES

13'

APPROX 4'

Side Elevation

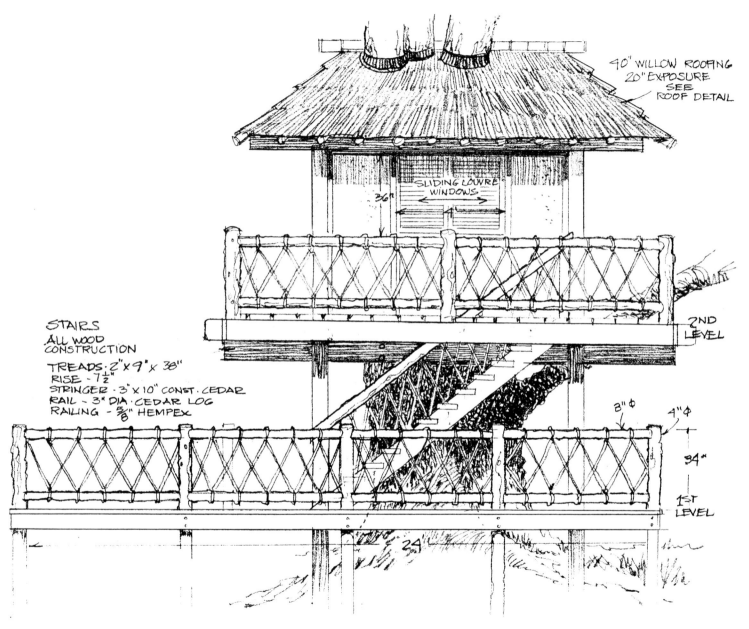

40" WILLOW ROOFING
20" EXPOSURE
SEE
ROOF DETAIL

SLIDING LOUVRE WINDOWS

36"

STAIRS

ALL WOOD
CONSTRUCTION

TREADS · 2" x 9" x 38"
RISE · 7½"
STRINGER · 3" x 10" CONST. CEDAR
RAIL · 3" DIA · CEDAR LOG
RAILING · ⅝" HEMPEX

2ND LEVEL

3"Φ   4"Φ

34"

1ST LEVEL

24"

Rear Elevation

timber-frame micro-barn

This tiny house nestles at the far end of a sloping back yard, and was specifically designed as a place to meditate, practice yoga, read, write and relax. The owners wanted a building large enough to sleep in. They hand-crafted a strong spiral stairway from found wood, leading to a sleeping loft whose circular window provides ventilation and a fine view. There's an armoire against the wall for storage; other than that, just a few essential books adorn the shelves under the recycled windows lining the walls.

The dimensions of the structure were determined by an existing cement base for an old shed. It made sense to use this foundation for our beautifully proportioned micro-barn. We used timber-frame construction through-out – carving out the notches of the traditional joints ourselves, using hand tools. Two people can assemble the completed frame in a couple of hours. After delivering the prepared and carefully marked pieces of lumber, we organized a "barn raising" party with the owners and their friends, and ended the day with a cookout.

Traditional timber-frame construction takes a little longer than conventional techniques, but the result is arguably stronger and there's undoubtedly a special sense of achievement once it's done – ask anyone who has tried it, and you'll find they are immensely proud of their accomplishment.

Timber framing continues the tradition of carpenters using handsaws, chisels and wooden mallets to create buildings that far outlast their own lifetimes. It uses less wood, but can produce a stronger building. When you walk into a timber-framed building there's a satisfaction in seeing the actual bones of the structure. Yes, the timber-frame method will take longer: to cut an accurate mortise and tenon might easily take half an hour, compared to the few minutes required to cut and nail two 2x4s; but if you can invest the time and interest, do consider it.

Unlike post and beam framing, which uses simple lap-joints and nails, timber framing is a centuries-old building technique for joining heavy timbers, the mortise and tenon joints being secured by oak pegs called "trunnels" (treenails). A trunnel is made by splitting a section off an oak block using a froe, and shaping it to a rough point with a hatchet. Diagonal braces are set into the posts and top plates, to keep the building from racking (bending) under strong winds.

Typically, a sharply pitched roof sheds rain and snow more easily, and also creates space for a loft.

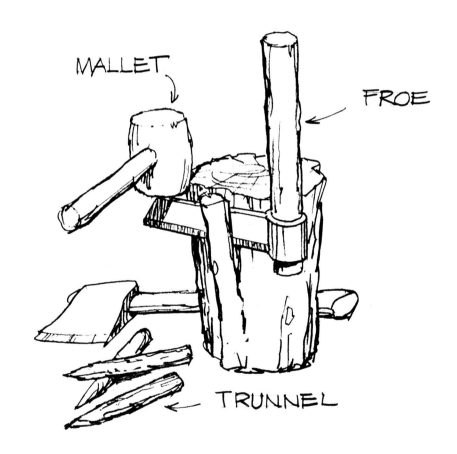

MALLET

FROE

TRUNNEL

TOOLS

The tools you will need for timber-framing are basically the same tools used by carpenters for centuries:

A - 1¼" wide framing chisel
B - 24" long framer's slick
C – Marking gauge
D – Standard wooden mallet
E – Combination square
F – Timber saw

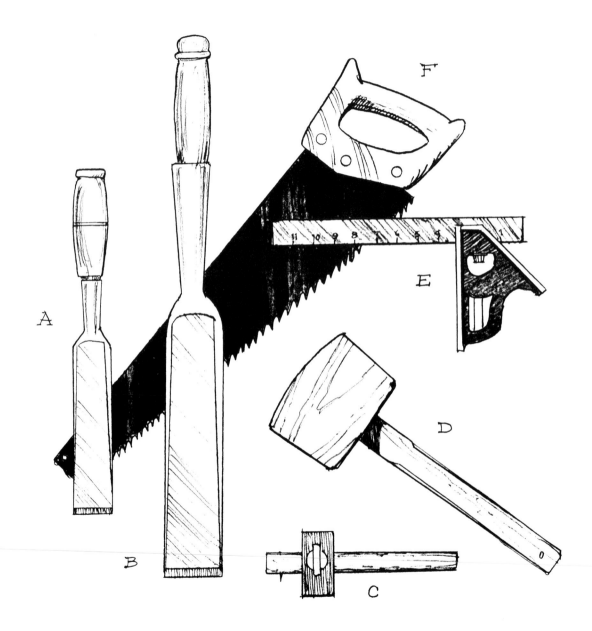

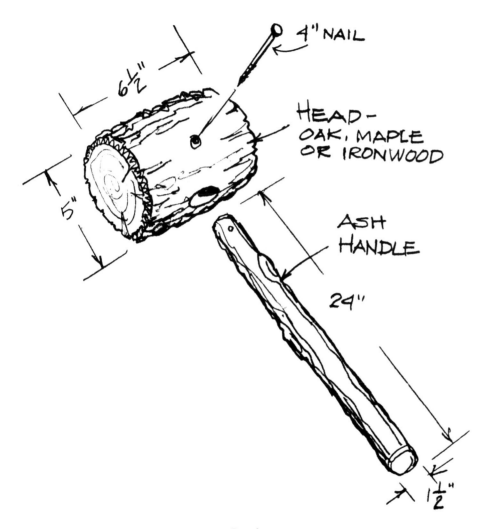

4" NAIL

$6\frac{1}{2}$"

HEAD —
OAK, MAPLE
OR IRONWOOD

5"

ASH
HANDLE

24"

$1\frac{1}{2}$"

Beetle

You will also need:

- Heavy home-made mallet (beetle or commander)
- Mason's line
- Mason's string level
- 4' long level
- Tape measure
- Framing square
- Carpenter's pencil
- Crosscut saw
- 7' stepladder

The only electric tool you might want (to make the job go faster) is a cordless drill for roughing out the mortise holes. The traditional tool is a hand-brace and bit, which also works perfectly well.

WOOD

Many professional timber framers recommend Northern Pine, because it is inexpensive, easy to cut, and not prone to shrink; we also like it because it smells so good once the building is finished. Of course, other types of wood are fine too – for instance, old barns were typically built of white oak to last forever. The only downside of oak is that it's twice as heavy as pine, which may be a factor especially if you are building on your own. The timber-framed barn we live in (which, at the time of writing, is supporting two feet of snow) was built 150 years ago using hemlock rafters that have stood the test of time (shown then [left] and now [right]).

HOW WE BUILT A TIMBER-FRAMED TINY HOUSE

Several years ago we were asked to design a small building that could be made and sold by the Amish in upstate New York. We came up with a simple, traditional, timber-framed cabin under 100 square feet (for easy transportation and installation).

We asked the Amish craftsmen to build a shed for our own use; it was shipped in pieces to Long Island, where we held a 'mini barn-raising' of our own using volunteers from the community. The event was a huge success and took place in an open field in the center of Amagansett, NY. To make it exciting for the kids, we made small wooden mallets and allowed them to help their parents hammer the trunnels.

Following the event, we had a call from someone who wanted us to build him a timber frame to replace a dilapidated shed on a concrete slab. Here is his description of what he wanted:

Being a native of New England, from a young age I have appreciated the simple, long-lasting and aesthetically beautiful design of the timber-frame barn. The timber-frame design is pure genius. Without room for a full-scale barn, we opted for a scaled-down version I like to call the "Micro-Barn." I wanted to include simple and utilitarian design elements like double Dutch doors, the sleeping loft, and our own spiral stair made out of wood from our yard, while keeping a 19th Century feel to the whole project. My motivation and vision for my Micro-Barn is simple: a quiet and inspiring place to read, write, think, and on occasion sip a nice scotch.

The owner sent us some sketches of how he wanted the barn to look; we developed them into workable construction drawings and a Materials List for the timber-framing, and ordered the rough-cut timbers from the Amish.

MATERIALS

Qty.	Description	Size	Location
Pressure-treated Lumber			
4	6x6	14'	sill plates
6	4x6	14'	floor joists
3	2x6	14'	girder (unless built on a concrete slab)
Rough-sawn Northern Pine			
4	5x5	8'	corner posts
4	5x6	14'	top plates
10	3x5	8'	studs
4	3x5	14'	girts
1	4x6	14'	loft support beam
3	4x6	14'	loft joists
2	4x4	12'	braces
14	3x5	12'	rafters
Tongue & groove fir			
29	2x6	14'	ground floor
15	2x6	14'	loft

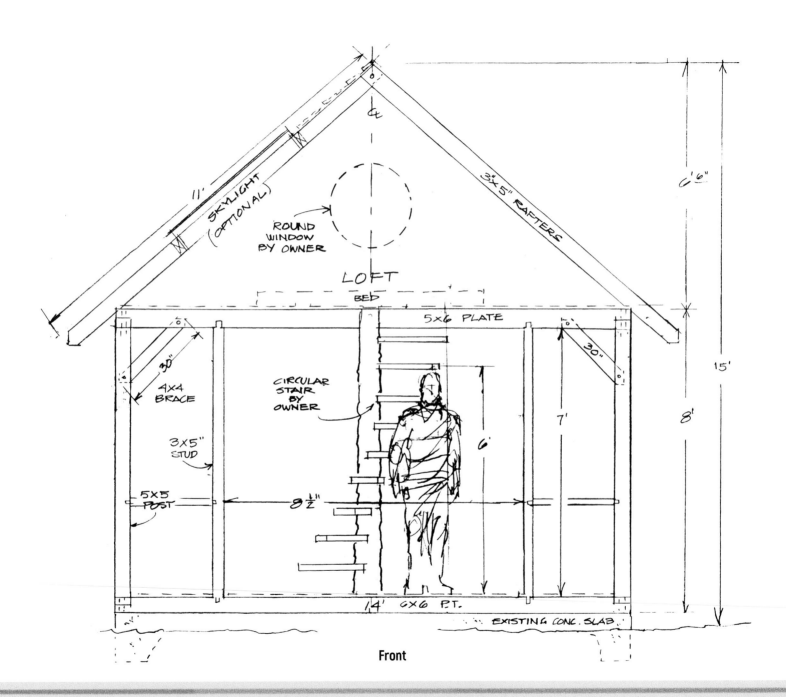

SKYLIGHT (OPTIONAL)

11'

3"X 5" RAFTERS

6"

ROUND WINDOW BY OWNER

LOFT

BED

5X6 PLATE

6'6"

15'

30"

4X4 BRACE

CIRCULAR STAIR BY OWNER

30"

7'

6'

3X5" STUD

8'

5X5 POST

8½"

14' 6X6 P.T.

EXISTING CONC. SLAB

Front

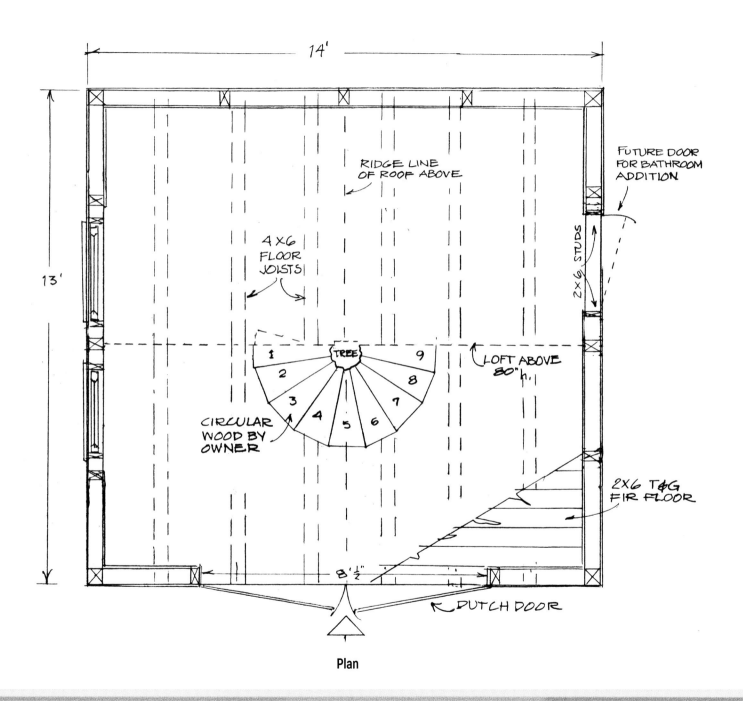

14'

13'

RIDGE LINE
OF ROOF ABOVE

FUTURE DOOR
FOR BATHROOM
ADDITION

4 X 6
FLOOR
JOISTS

2 X 6 STUDS

1   TREE   9

2   8

3   7

4   5   6

LOFT ABOVE
80" h.

CIRCULAR
WOOD BY
OWNER

2X6 T&G
FIR FLOOR

8'½"

DUTCH DOOR

Plan

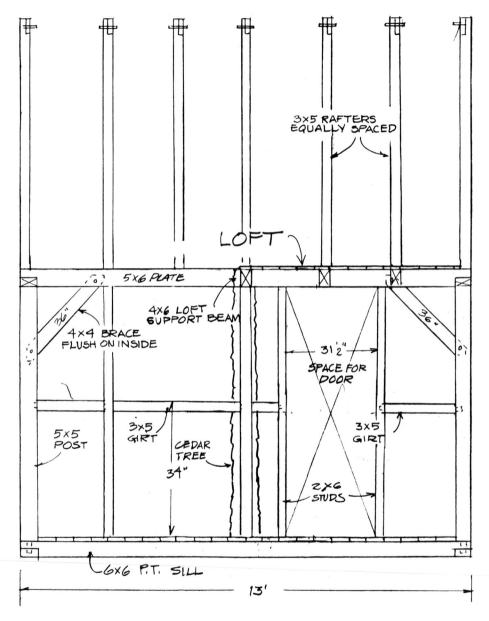

3X5 RAFTERS EQUALLY SPACED

LOFT

5X6 PLATE

4X6 LOFT SUPPORT BEAM

36"

4X4 BRACE FLUSH ON INSIDE

31' 2" SPACE FOR DOOR

5X5 POST

3X5 GIRT

CEDAR TREE 34"

3X5 GIRT

2X6 STUDS

6X6 P.T. SILL

13'

Right Side

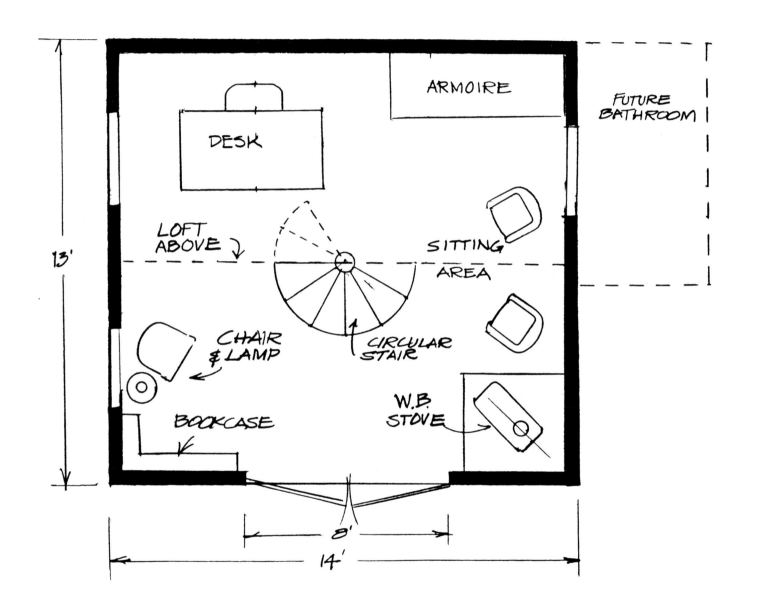

ARMOIRE

FUTURE
BATHROOM

DESK

LOFT
ABOVE

SITTING
AREA

CHAIR
& LAMP

CIRCULAR
STAIR

W.B.
STOVE

BOOKCASE

13'

8'

14'

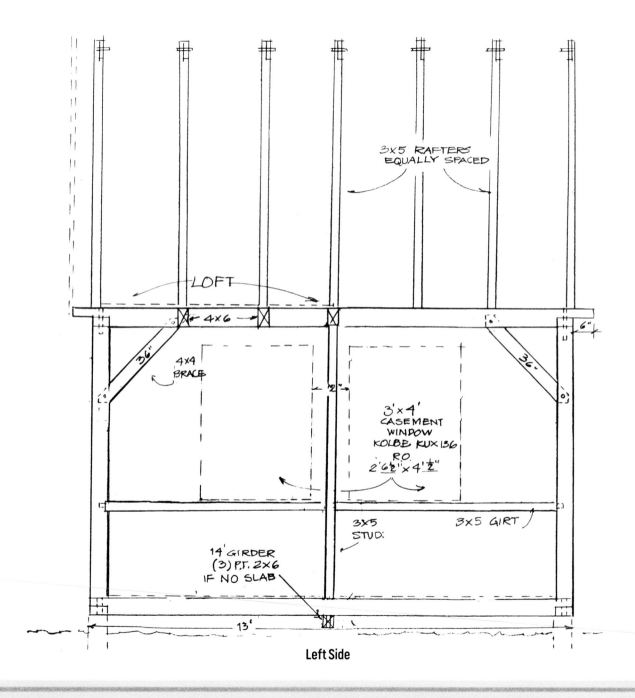

3X5 RAFTERS
EQUALLY SPACED

LOFT

4X6

3X5 STUDS

4X4 BRACE

36"

36"

6"

2"

3'x4'
CASEMENT
WINDOW
KOLBE KUX136
R.O.
2'6½"x4'½"

3X5 GIRT

14' GIRDER
(3) P.T. 2x6
IF NO SLAB

13'

Left Side

When the timbers arrived at our shop, we stacked them in order of their use, and making sure they were protected from rain. (The lumber had been kiln-dried for several months prior to shipping.)

We began by removing vegetation, rocks and stumps from an area of the yard, and made the ground reasonably flat. We set stakes to mark the corners of the building, double-checking that the diagonals were equal so the building would be square (see below).

We set leveled concrete blocks at the corners; it's important to tamp down the soil under the blocks before setting them, to prevent the building from sinking as the weight increases.

The first beams to put in place were the heavy 6x6 pressure-treated sill beams. We cut them to length and joined the ends with lap joints (shown page 102, top left). Next, we cut 2"x2" mortise holes through both

pieces using first a wood drill and then a framing chisel. To ensure that the holes were centered, we made a cardboard template to use on all the subsequent holes. We also cut spare pieces (test blocks) of 2"x2", both to check the fit of each mortise and to hold the corners together during the next phase of construction. The post tenon is 5" long (page 102, bottom left).

We cut the six 4x6 pressure-treated floor joists to length and shaped them with a chisel to fit into a dovetail mortise in the 6x6 sill plate. You can see in the drawing that the bottom of the joist is cut at an angle; this is to reduce stress on the beam. The pocket cut in the sill plates must be carefully adjusted so that the joists don't rest too high or too low for the future floorboards (see sill plate/floor joist detail on page 102).

The four 5" x 5" corner posts have 2" x 2" x 5" tenons on each end to fit into the sill

plates and top plates. At this point we decided it would be difficult to keep lifting the top plates over the corner posts to test them for fit; instead we decided to set the top plates temporarily upside-down on top of the leveled sill plates, and cut the mortises. With the timbers conveniently on the ground, we also cut all the mortises for the 3x5 wall studs, the horizontal girts and the 4x4 braces. This was kind of tricky because we had to keep reminding ourselves how the timbers would be positioned when the building finally went together. You need good spatial awareness and careful labeling for this stage.

The 4x4 braces required special mortises to fit the corner posts and top plates (see page 103). You may notice that the braces are different lengths where they meet at the corner posts – this avoids the potential weak spot caused by two joints at the same point.

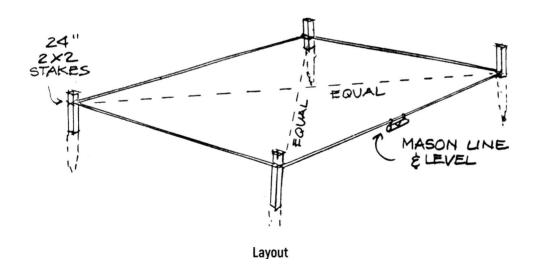

Layout

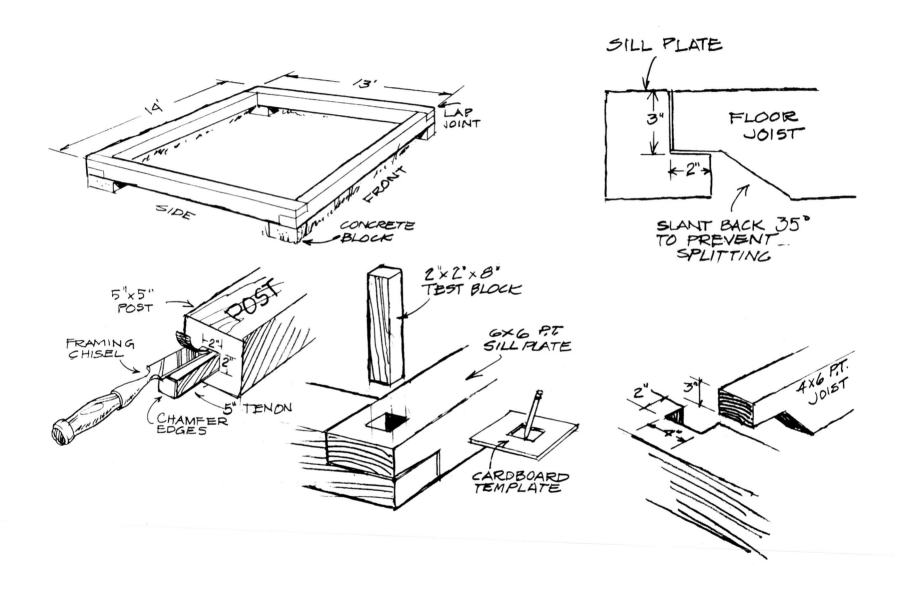

14'

13'

LAP JOINT

SIDE

FRONT

CONCRETE BLOCK

SILL PLATE

3"

2"

FLOOR JOIST

SLANT BACK 35° TO PREVENT SPLITTING

5"×5" POST

POST

FRAMING CHISEL

2"

2"

5" TENON

CHAMFER EDGES

2"×2"×8" TEST BLOCK

6×6 P.T. SILL PLATE

CARDBOARD TEMPLATE

2"

3"

4"

4×6 P.T. JOIST

Once all the mortises and tenons were cut, we put the whole frame together for a trial fit (see page 104, left).

The next job was to cut and fit the three joists supporting the loft. Since these beams also help prevent the side walls from spreading, we dovetailed the ends (see Loft Dovetail Joint sketch on page 105).

With the structure standing, we cut a pair of rafters. We joined them at the top with a pegged lap joint, and cut a bird's-mouth joint where they met the top plates (see page 104, right). We screwed a temporary cross-piece to the rafters and lifted them into place as a single unit; once we were sure of the fit, we cut the remaining rafters using the first pair as a pattern. We held the end rafters in place by attaching a 16' long 2x4 'mast' to the top and bottom plates, and fastening the rafters to this (see page 105). Once these were set, we attached a temporary 1x6 board between the two pairs of rafters to secure them. We marked the 1x6 and the top plates where the additional rafters were to go. We made five more rafter sets and lifted them into place.

The completed timber frame was dismantled, stacked onto a truck and driven to the site, where a barn-raising was organized. We all helped put it back together in a matter of a few hours, and were rewarded with a delicious meal and drinks. It took the owner about a year, working weekends, to finish the micro-barn: installing recycled windows, building a loft, wooden circular stairs, and creating a unique getaway for himself. He has plans for a wood stove and then a mini commode in the future.

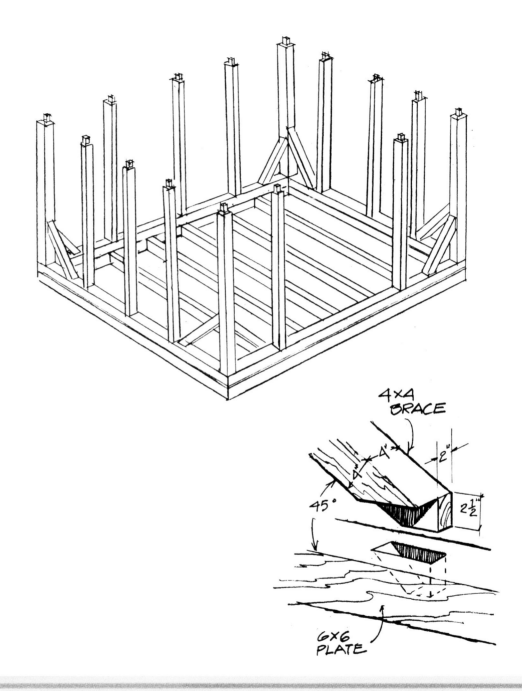

4×4 BRACE

4"

4"

2"

45°

2½"

6×6 PLATE

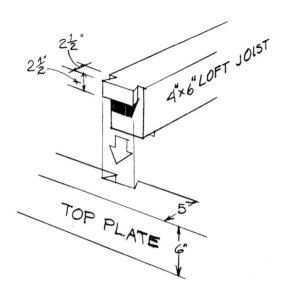

2½"
2½"

4"×6" LOFT JOIST

TOP PLATE

5"

6"

Loft Dovetail Joint

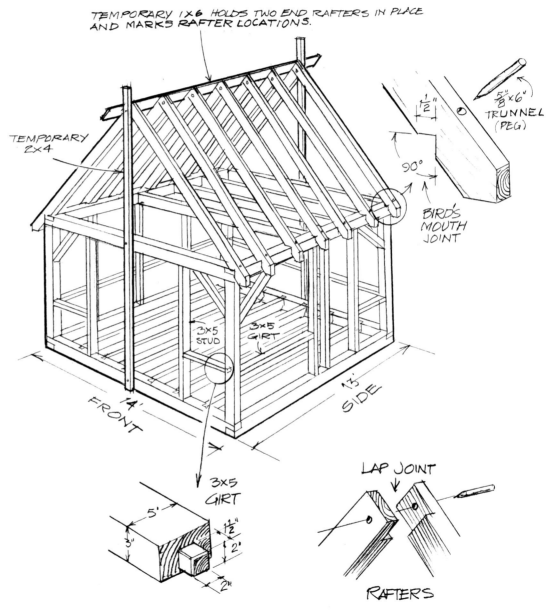

TEMPORARY 1×6 HOLDS TWO END RAFTERS IN PLACE AND MARKS RAFTER LOCATIONS.

TEMPORARY 2×4

1½"

90°

⅝"×6" TRUNNEL (PEG)

BIRD'S MOUTH JOINT

3×5 STUD

3×5 GIRT

14' FRONT

13' SIDE

3×5 GIRT

5'

3"

1½"

2'

2"

LAP JOINT

RAFTERS

TIMBER-FRAME TIPS

When drawing up plans, use 2 squares to a foot for a small building, one square to a foot for a larger one (¼" grid paper works well). It makes sense to place the door at the highest point of the building site.

Anything in contact with the ground (such as sill plates and floor joists) should be pressure-treated wood.

We cut the larger joints using a coarse-cut handsaw. We recommend the Bahco Profcut and Superior saws. A large chisel or framer's slick is also useful for lap joints and for finishing tenons (such as the tenon shown on page 108).

Find and mark the center of timbers, tenons and mortises, using a marking gauge. We made a simple cardboard template to speed up the process of marking identical mortises, and used a dummy tenon made from a scrap of wood to test each one for fit.

Cut temporary pegs to hold the finished sills together while you set them in place with the help of a level and framing square (and blocks if necessary). Always check that the diagonals are equal.

Number the joints systematically as you work so you can identify them when you assemble the frame. Use a permanent marker or chisel. Accurate measurements are critical so don't just assume joints fit – make sure to check them!

We designed this tiny house to have vertical sheathing or texture 111- grooved plywood, nailed to the outside of the frame. For horizontal cladding, add 2x4 vertical studs, 24" apart. You can insulate between the studs and cover with drywall.

sugar cube house

The idea for the Sugar Cube House came from a study popularized by the media in 2016, claiming that 32 percent of millennials lived at home with their parents. Some families may be quite happy about this, but it's not ideal for young people who want the independence of their own home.

We envisioned the house as a home for someone just starting out in life – perhaps a college graduate with limited funds and a big loan to pay off – but the design would work equally well for anyone wanting their own space on a budget. The start-up Cube 1 might initially be built on borrowed land (such as a friend's property or parents' backyard), and moved when the owner becomes more established: the design allows it to be unbolted and shipped to a new location if required. A more permanent home evolves as cubes are added.

Key features of The Sugar Cube House:

- Inexpensive – material cost of each cube (room) is approximately $2000. (2016)
- Easy to build, with modular panel construction
- More like a real house – unlike many tiny houses
- Can be dismantled and moved on a flatbed truck
- Designed to grow: one, two or three cubes
- Efficient use of materials helps to minimize waste
- Good cross-ventilation from window placement
- Can be used off-grid using solar, a composting toilet and a wood stove
- Rain catchment system for bathing and washing
- Passive solar gain through large sliding glass doors
- Outdoor covered patio/eating area
- Suitable for temporary or permanent foundation
- Additional cubes can be added as needed
- Patio can be screened in or enclosed

Backyard temporary living quarters:
- Foundation: concrete blocks
- Heat: electric or propane gas heater
- Lights: extension cord from house
- Water: garden hose, bottled water
- WC: main house or Loveable Loo (see Resources, page 201)
- Bathing: main house
- Cooking: double hot plate, microwave and mini refrigerator

Off-grid location (semi-permanent):
- Foundation: insulated (see Foundations, page 17)
- Heat: passive solar heating and wood burning stove
- Lights: solar panels and gas wall lights
- Water: rain catchment system and bottled water
- WC: composting toilet
- Cooking: propane gas cooking unit and icebox or gas refrigerator

Permanent dwelling:
- Foundation: post and skirt
- Bathing: bath with shower using on-demand water heater
- Heat: electric or gas
- Lights: electric and solar
- Water: private well
- WC: approved septic system
- Cooking: full-size gas oven and electric refrigerator

CUBE 1 – SINGLE ROOM CUBE

Cube 1 will comfortably accommodate one person on a temporary basis; it stands on concrete blocks so it can be easily moved to a new location. The design includes a mini kitchen (see Avanti Mini Kitchens or Dwyer) which includes a sink (A), two gas burners, and a small refrigerator (B). Storage is provided by wall cabinets (C) on two sides, and by pullout drawers under the 30" x 69" bed (D). A table (E) serves as both a desk and dining area, with storage (F) above for files, a TV, etc.

Heat comes from a propane gas wall heater (G) *(see Heating, page 130)*. The toilet can be a simple "Loveable Loo" which must be emptied every few days, or a more elaborate composting toilet *(see Toilets, page 142)*.

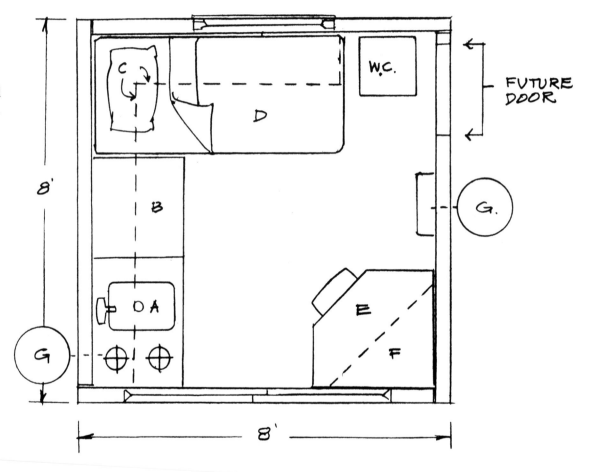

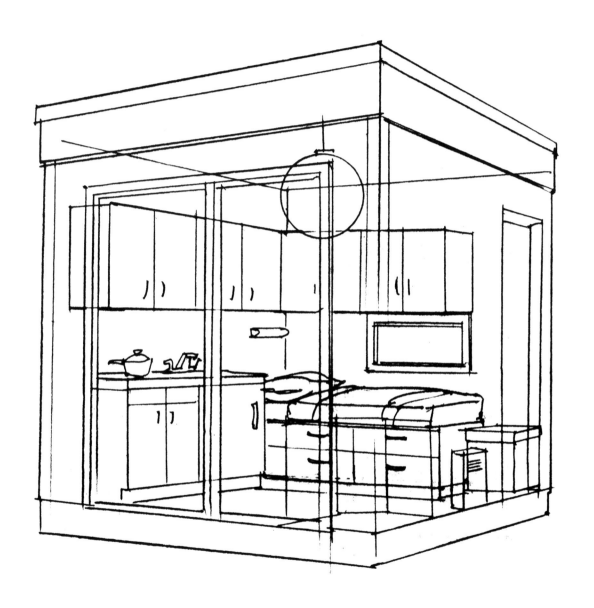

CUBE 2 – BEDROOM/LIVING ROOM

Cube 2 moves the bed out of the kitchen and provides room for sleep, work and relaxation; it will also become the main entrance for the Sugar Cube House and provide a passageway (G) between the kitchen and bathroom when all three units are built. The sliding glass doors can be fitted with shades for privacy *(see Resources, page 201)*.

The bed (A) is built-in. The bed is built over two rollout storage drawers.

Next to the foot of the bed is a 22" deep x 24" wide closet (B) for hanging clothes.

Next to the head of the bed is a built-in desk (C).

A built-in storage unit, with shelves and space ideal for a computer or TV, extends across the wall behind the desk and bed (D).

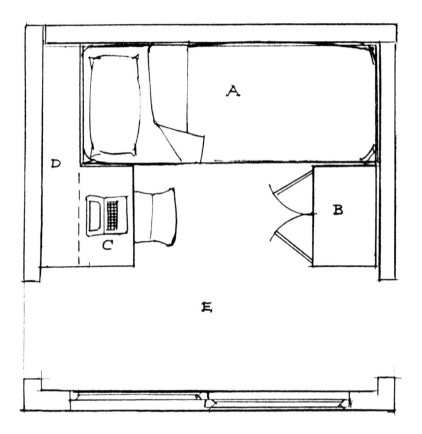

CUBE 3 – BATHROOM

Cube 3 is designed for a more permanent location, where the owner wants a full bathroom. It is connected to electricity, water and an approved septic system. The 6" plumbing wall (A) allows easy access to the plumbing fixtures. Hot and cold water lines run under the floor to the other side of the room. The full-size bathtub (B) and shower with drain are tied into an approved septic system. The vanity cabinet (C) is 3' wide, with a faucet and marble counter *(see Resources, page 201)*. The mirrored wall cabinet (D) has a built-in light *(see Resources)*. Above the washing machine (E) is a storage cabinet; the towel rack (F) and gas-fired (or equivalent) heater (G) are wall-mounted. The toilet (H) can be of composting or standard type. An on-demand gas water heater (I) is attached to the plumbing wall.

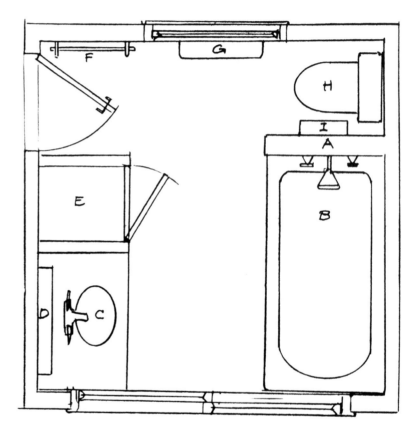

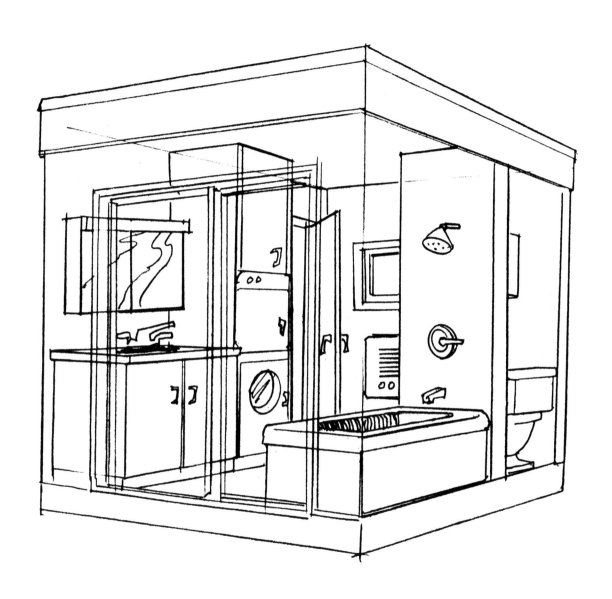

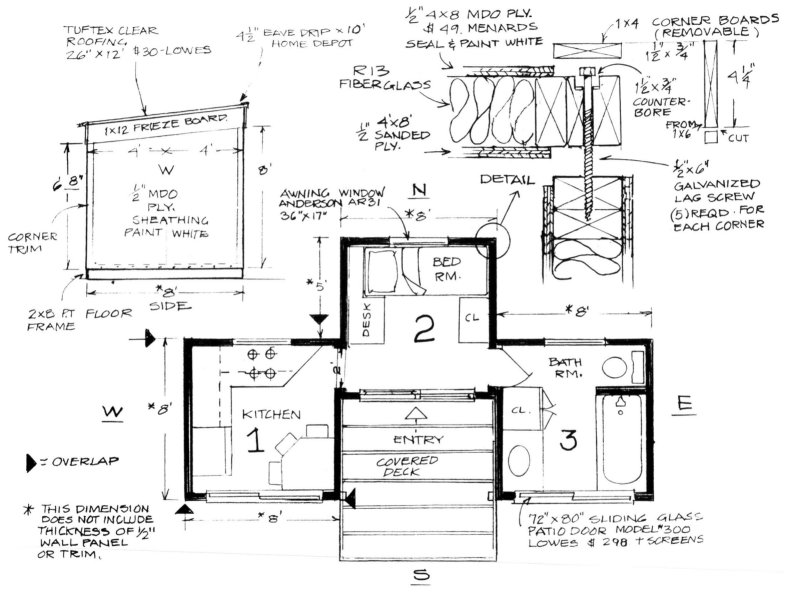

TUFTEX CLEAR ROOFING. 26" × 12' #30-LOWES

4½" EAVE DRIP × 10' HOME DEPOT

½" 4×8 MDO PLY. # 49. MENARDS SEAL & PAINT WHITE

1×4 CORNER BOARDS (REMOVABLE)

1" × ¾"
1½ × ¾

4¼"

R13 FIBERGLASS

1½ × ¾" COUNTER-BORE

FROM 1×6

CUT

1×12 FRIEZE BOARD.

½" 4×8' SANDED PLY.

4' × 4'

W

½" MDO. PLY. SHEATHING PAINT WHITE

6' 8"

8'

½"×6" GALVANIZED LAG SCREW (5) REQD. FOR EACH CORNER

CORNER TRIM

AWNING WINDOW ANDERSON AR31 36"×17"

N

* 8'

DETAIL

* 8'

SIDE

2×8 P.T FLOOR FRAME

* 5'

BED RM.

2

CL

* 8'

W

* 8'

DESK

KITCHEN

1

BATH RM.

ENTRY

CL.

3

COVERED DECK

E

▶ = OVERLAP

* 8'

* THIS DIMENSION DOES NOT INCLUDE THICKNESS OF ½" WALL PANEL OR TRIM.

72"×80" SLIDING GLASS PATIO DOOR MODEL#300 LOWES $ 298 +SCREENS

S

Sugar Cube House Plan

BUILDING THE CUBES

Throughout the construction of the Sugar Cube House, mark each piece South, West, North or East. This makes it easier to remember where each piece goes, especially when moving and reassembling them.

Begin by leveling the site as much as possible, and stake out the 8' square area for the cube house.

If you are using a temporary foundation of concrete blocks, use a level to determine how many blocks you will need at the corners, and ensure they are tamped firmly into the ground.

For a more permanent foundation (see Foundations, page 17), dig 30"-36" deep holes at the corners and at the halfway points. This will give you a surface to attach cement board at 4' intervals. Set the posts in 1½" from the perimeter to allow for the thickness of the 2x8 floor beams. Build the floor platform as shown by cutting four 2x8 pressure treated (P.T.) boards 94½" long and nail them together, using #10 galvanized common nails, to form an 8' square. Cut five 2x8 P.T. boards, 93" long, and nail them at 16" intervals to the front and rear perimeter beams.

Cover the floor frame with two sheets of ¾" AC plywood, screwed to the joists using 1½" screws.

Floor Platform

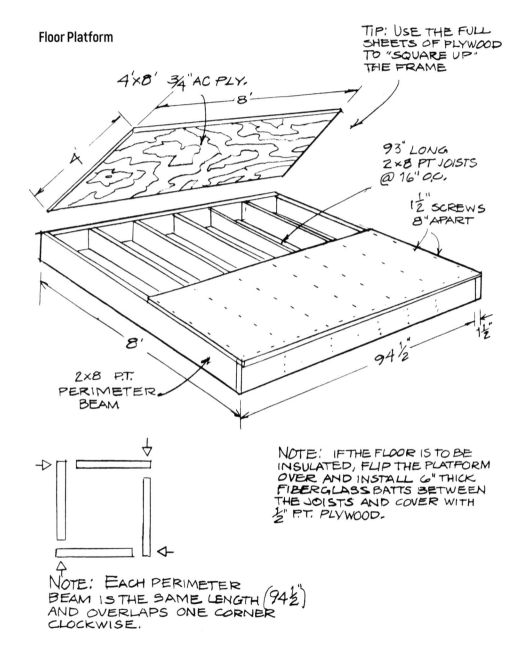

4'x8' ¾" AC PLY.

8'

4'

TIP: USE THE FULL SHEETS OF PLYWOOD TO "SQUARE UP" THE FRAME

93" LONG 2x8 PT JOISTS @ 16" O.C.

1½" SCREWS 8" APART

8'

94½"

1½"

2x8 P.T. PERIMETER BEAM

NOTE: IF THE FLOOR IS TO BE INSULATED, FLIP THE PLATFORM OVER AND INSTALL 6" THICK FIBERGLASS BATTS BETWEEN THE JOISTS AND COVER WITH ½" P.T. PLYWOOD.

NOTE: EACH PERIMETER BEAM IS THE SAME LENGTH (94½") AND OVERLAPS ONE CORNER CLOCKWISE.

WALL FRAMING

The wall panels are joined at the corners in clockwise fashion (see Corner Detail, page 118), with five ½" x 6" galvanized lag screws per corner. The framing studs at the corners are doubled or tripled for strength. The figure shown here and those on pages 121 and 122 show placement of the studs; but think about where you might want doorways later if you plan to add more cubes, and adjust stud spacing accordingly. Once the walls are framed, cover the exterior with MDO plywood *(see Resources – Menards, page 201)*; this weighs over 40 lbs. per sheet, so it will require two people to install. Highway departments use it for signs, as it is very durable and a good base for paint; each cube only needs seven sheets, and you can cover all the walls for $350 (2016). Seal the edges and all joints with white silicone caulking during assembly. Use (white) 2" paneling nails to attach the MDO board to the studs; apply a bead of polyurethane adhesive to the studs before nailing. Note that each exterior panel extends 3" below the bottom of the framing – this provides a lip to screw the wall to the floor platform. Be careful not to paint the screw heads, as you'll need to undo them if you ever want to disassemble the building and move it.

Depending on climate, you may want to insulate the walls and ceiling; in northern states you may even want to insulate the floor.

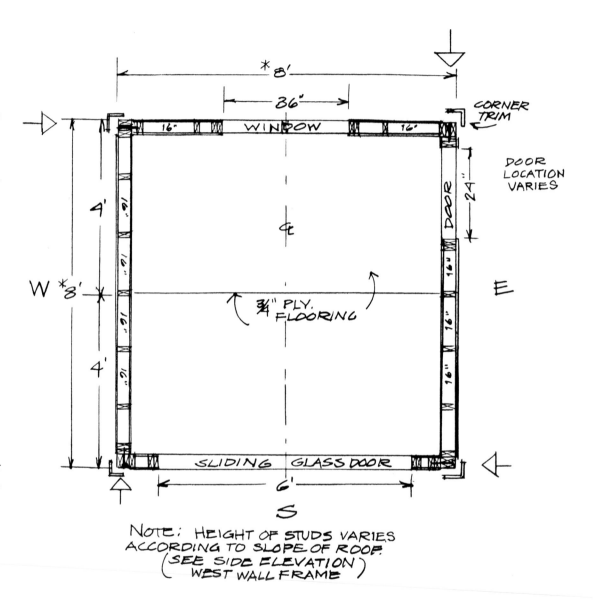

Typical 2 x 4 Wall Stud Framing

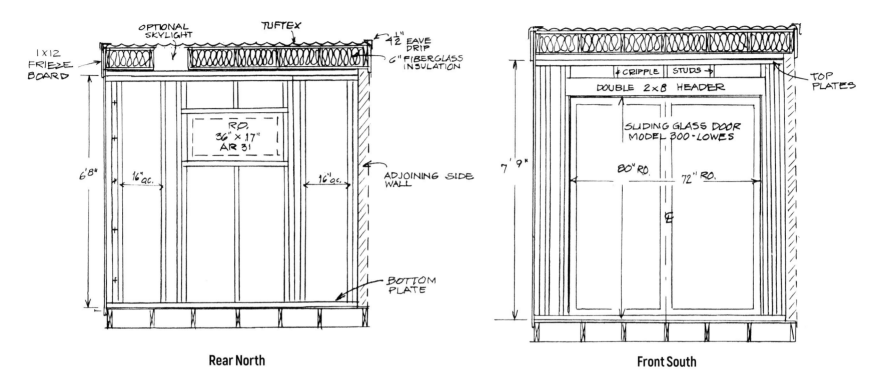

Rear North

Front South

The interior of the cube is covered with ½" sanded plywood. This lightweight product has a smooth surface that is easily painted. Use white annular paneling nails to attach the plywood to the interior studs.

As you finish the panels, stack them close to the site ready for assembly. They'll be heavy and you will need some help here. It will only take a day to put it all together, so why not have a Sugar Cube party?

WALL INSTALLATION

It will take at least three people to lift the panels into place. Temporarily brace each panel upright until all four are securely joined. Counter-bore five equidistant 1½" diameter holes ¾" deep in the tripled end studs – the center of the holes should be 1¾" from the end of the wall; follow with ½" pilot holes drilled completely through the studs. Using the ½" holes as a guide, drill ⅜" holes through the doubled studs in the adjoining panel. Join the panels using a socket wrench and ½" x 6" galvanized lag screws.

The corner boards should withstand several removals and refits (if the cubes get relocated). Attach the boards using #10 (2½") washer-head screws *(see Resources, page 201)*

about 14" apart on both sides of the corner. Be careful not to cover the screw heads with paint or you may be sorry later.

ROOF

The roof is built much like the floor except that the ends of the ceiling joists are cut off at a 9° slant (see page 122). You can mark the angle on the side beams and joists using the slope of the side wall (while it's lying flat) as a guide; cut them shorter to allow for the thickness of the front and rear beams (3" in total), which overlap the side beams. Join the four perimeter beams using three screws

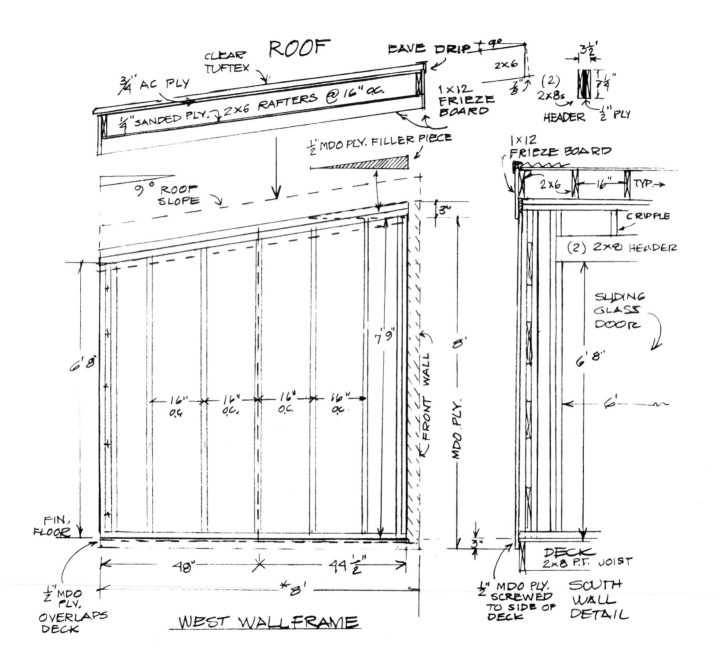

ROOF

CLEAR TUFTEX

EAVE DRIP

¾" AC PLY

¼" SANDED PLY. 2X6 RAFTERS @ 16" O.C.

1X12 FRIEZE BOARD

9°

2X6

⅛"

(2) 2X8s

3½"

7¼"

HEADER

½" PLY

½" MDO PLY. FILLER PIECE

9° ROOF SLOPE

1X12 FRIEZE BOARD

2X6

16"

TYP.

CRIPPLE

(2) 2X8 HEADER

3"

SLIDING GLASS DOOR

7'9"

6'8"

6'8"

6'

8'

FRONT WALL

MDO. PLY.

16" O.C.   16" O.C.   16" O.C.   16" O.C.

FIN. FLOOR

3"

DECK
2X8 P.T. JOIST

½" MDO PLY. OVERLAPS DECK

48"

44½"

*8'

½" MDO PLY. SCREWED TO SIDE OF DECK

WEST WALL FRAME

SOUTH WALL DETAIL

MATERIALS

Qty.	Description	Size
FLOOR PLATFORM		
9	2x8 P.T. lumber	18'
2	¾" AC plywood	4' x 8'
	Nails	
	Screws	
WALLS		
55	2x4 spruce	8'
7	½" MDO plywood	4' x 8'
7	½" sanded plywood	4' x 8'
	Nails	
	Screws	
	Paneling nails	
	½" x 6" galv. lag screws	
ROOF		
9	2x6 spruce	8'
2	¾" AC plywood	4' x 8'
2	¼" sanded plywood	4' x 8'
4	Clear Tuftex	12'
4	1x12 #2 pine	12' (frieze)
	Screws	
	6d nails	
	1 box Tuftex fasteners	
LOUVERED PERGOLA		
9	2x6 #2 fir	8'
2	4x4 P.T. lumber	8'
	½" x 5" galv. lag screws	
	½" washers	

MISCELLANEOUS	
	adhesive, caulking, drip edge, doors, windows
INSULATION	
120 ft.	3½" fiberglass rolls (walls)
48 ft.	6" fiberglass rolls (roof)

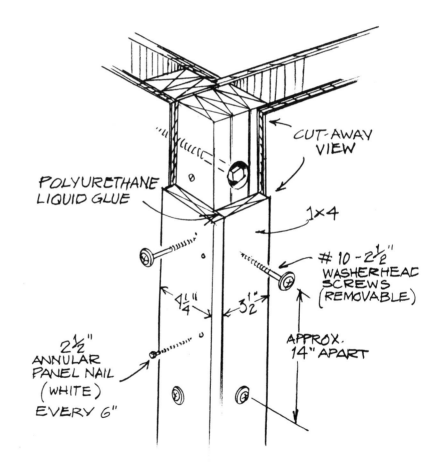

POLYURETHANE LIQUID GLUE

CUT-AWAY VIEW

1x4

#10 - 2½" WASHERHEAD SCREWS (REMOVABLE)

APPROX. 14" APART

2½" ANNULAR PANEL NAIL (WHITE) EVERY 6"

4¼"

3½"

per corner. Make a center mark (at 48") on the front and rear beams and mark at 16" intervals across the beams to locate where the ceiling joists should go. Screw the joists to the front and rear beams, using three screws from the outside and four toenailed on the inside. Cover the roof with two sheets of ¾" AC plywood fastened with #6 galvanized common nails; the two sheets of plywood won't quite cover the joists, so mark and cut an extra strip to fit at the top. Line the inside with ¼" sanded plywood. Cover the plywood roof with four sheets of 26" x 12' Tuftex carbonate corrugated roofing *(see Resources – Lowes, page 201)*, following the manufacturer's installation guidelines.

A skylight can be easily built in any of the cubes by boxing in-between two ceiling joists and making a cutout in both layers of plywood before installing the corrugated roofing. The clear Tuftex will keep out the rain but let in plenty of light.

FRIEZE BOARD

"Frieze" is a classical architectural term given to a horizontal band below the roof, sometimes elaborately decorated as in the Parthenon; in our more modest Sugar Cube House, it joins the roof to the walls. Use the same washer-head screws so it can be detached at a later date.

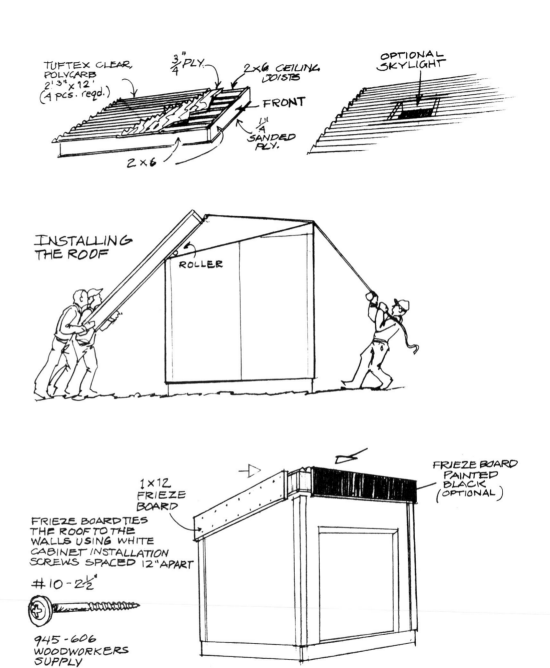

TUFTEX CLEAR, POLYCARB 2'3" X 12' (4 pcs. reqd.)

¾" PLY.

2×6 CEILING JOISTS

OPTIONAL SKYLIGHT

FRONT

¼" SANDED PLY.

2×6

INSTALLING THE ROOF

ROLLER

1×12 FRIEZE BOARD

FRIEZE BOARD PAINTED BLACK (OPTIONAL)

FRIEZE BOARD TIES THE ROOF TO THE WALLS USING WHITE CABINET INSTALLATION SCREWS SPACED 12" APART

#10 - 2½"

945 - 606 WOODWORKERS SUPPLY

LOUVERED PERGOLA

An outdoor seating area between Cubes 1 and 2 forms a patio and outdoor dining area. The louvered pergola provides shade, adjustable by turning the 2x6 louvers with a homemade plywood wrench. Fit screens to the pergola if mosquitoes are a problem, or even wall it in to provide an extra room. If space allows, an extra door could be made in the kitchen wall to smooth the way from oven to table.

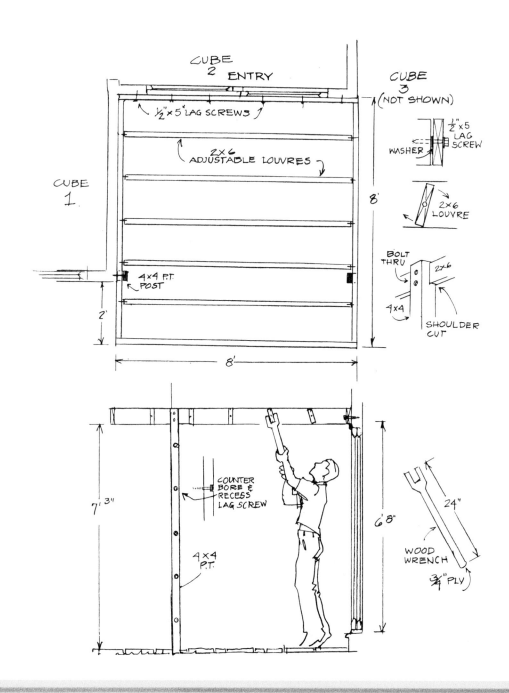

TWO | **finishing the interior**

lighting

There are several ways to light your house at night, depending on your circumstances. If you live off-grid you can use good old-fashioned candles or kerosene/white gas lamps – but with suitable precautions: any lantern or candle with an exposed flame will use up some of the oxygen in the house, so rooms must be adequately ventilated. Use caution when refueling and lighting this type of lamp: for example, never attempt to refill a portable lantern that has just run out of oil and is still hot – instead, make a habit of checking fuel levels during the daytime, when it's easier and safer.

Another choice is propane gas, as used by many Amish communities. These gas lights are the equivalent of 65 watts; they should be installed by a licensed plumber using ⅜" copper tubing. Gas lamps need a bit of TLC – cleaning the glass and sometimes replacing the fragile mantle – to keep them working well. The same applies to their kerosene or white gas equivalents *(see Resources – Lighting, page 201).*

A modern alternative is solar-powered lights. There are now many types on the market. You could incorporate skylights into your tiny house design. Place them over the kitchen sink or over your desk to optimize the charging of the solar panels. This will of course give you more light during the day as well. Some solar light fixtures come with a remote switch, so you can hang the light wherever you want and position the

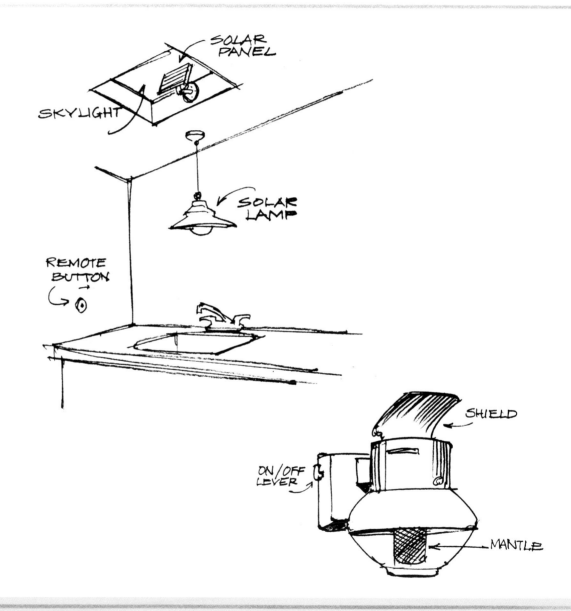

SOLAR PANEL

SKYLIGHT

SOLAR LAMP

REMOTE BUTTON

SHIELD

ON/OFF LEVER

MANTLE

solar panel to receive maximum sunlight *(see Resources – Solar Lighting, page 201).* Some lamps provide 25 lumens of light – roughly equivalent to a 25-watt bulb.

A SOLAR SYSTEM

The next time you look up at the sun, take a moment to consider it as a source of energy you can harness to run not just your lights, but also your refrigerator, TV, computer, phone and other devices. No wonder governments all over the world are spending huge amounts of money to prepare for a "solar" future. Solar is less costly to install than other sustainable sources of electricity such as wind generators and hydroelectric generators.

According to www.conserve-energy-future.com solar energy is:

- A clean energy source
- Renewable and sustainable
- Able to supply electricity to remote areas
- Readily installed on your rooftop
- Available forever, unlike the world's oil reserves
- Silent and non-polluting

At the time of this writing, the initial cost of installing solar power remains high; tax incentives can reduce the overall cost but it still takes a long time to break even. You should clean the panels once or twice a month, and the batteries must be topped up periodically. The batteries, which store energy for use overnight and during cloudy days, are heavy and need replacing after a few years. This may well change in the not-too distant future as technology develops.

HOW IT WORKS

Solar panels absorb sunlight through photovoltaic cells during the day in the form of DC current and send it to an inverter, which converts it into AC current. Some RVs and boats use the DC direct current, thereby omitting the inverter, but in this case all the electrical equipment must be DC compatible – often much more expensive. That said, eliminating the inverter decreases the cost of the installation and eliminates the noise of the fan in the inverter. In addition to the inverter, you will need a charge regulator, to prevent overcharging or undercharging the batteries.

Solar energy is measured in kilowatt hours (1 kilowatt = 1000 watts, or ten 100-watt light bulbs).

A modest solar-powered system for a tiny house might be approximately 250 watts. Estimate how many watts you will need to run your house.

Examples:

Laptop	120 watts
Refrigerator *	83 watts
Radio	7 watts
Cell phone recharger	4 watts
36-watt light bulb CFL	36 watts
	————
	250 watts

Refrigerator source: Avanti 1.7 cu f. 83 watts, 115v.

ADJUSTABLE SOLAR-PANEL RACK

The optimum angle for a solar array is at 90° to the sun. Large commercial solar installations accomplish this with motors that turn the panels to track the sun's path; you can do this more simply, by making this adjustable rack to follow the sun. Granted you won't want to spend all day rushing outside to adjust the angles, but if your batteries are low you might need to get every bit of solar energy you can – after a prolonged spell of cloudy weather, for example.

It only takes a few pieces of stock lumber and some stationary castors to make the turntable. The 1x4 supports tilt back and forth as required, like a lawn chair.

Adjustable Solar Panel Rack

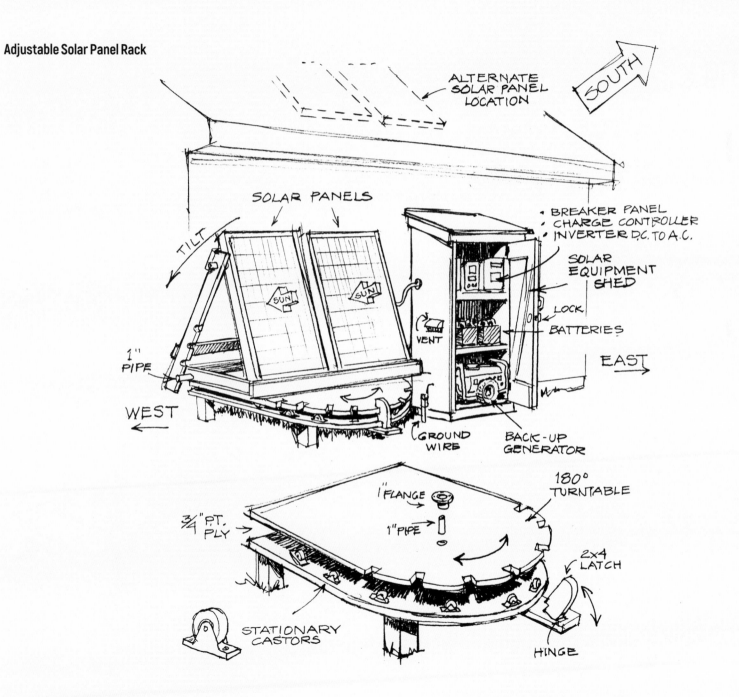

ALTERNATE SOLAR PANEL LOCATION

SOUTH

SOLAR PANELS

TILT

SUN

SUN

1" PIPE

WEST

VENT

GROUND WIRE

BREAKER PANEL
CHARGE CONTROLLER
INVERTER D.C. TO A.C.

SOLAR EQUIPMENT SHED

LOCK

BATTERIES

EAST

BACK-UP GENERATOR

1" FLANGE

180° TURNTABLE

1" PIPE

3/4" P.T. PLY

2x4 LATCH

STATIONARY CASTORS

HINGE

heating

The type of heating you choose for your tiny house (or office, workshop, studio, etc.) will depend on several factors, but the main one will be what type of fuel you have available: wood, propane or electric.

WOOD

The best wood to burn in a fireplace or wood-burning stove is hardwood such as oak, maple or hickory because they're long-burning. You've probably heard the old expression: "Wood heats you twice: once when you cut it and once when you burn it," which is true because it takes a lot of work to cut and split enough firewood to last a winter – perhaps 3-5 cords* depending on your situation. (A small house, of course, takes less fuel to heat.) If you buy from a supplier, make sure the logs have been seasoned for at least a year – preferably more – which you can tell from the lighter weight and the grey color. Some say it takes a year per inch (thickness) to season wood properly. One notable exception is ash, which burns well even when newly cut: "Sear or green, it's fit for a queen." A friend who heated his off-grid house entirely with wood for seventeen years confirms this; he also pointed out that its straight grain makes ash wood easy to split.

If you are going to cut and split your own wood, make it the right size for your stove or fireplace at the outset – this will hasten the seasoning process, and save time and effort later; also, smaller pieces tend to burn more efficiently. When splitting logs, we find that

standing them on end inside an old car tire helps keep them upright as you move around the stack wailing away at it. Store the wood in a covered shed open to the sun.

*A cord of firewood measures 4'x4'x8' – roughly the capacity of a small pick-up.

FIREWOOD STORAGE BOX

Consider adding the firewood box on page 131 to the outside of your tiny house. The box conveniently stores firewood so you can feed the stove without going outdoors; the door can be locked from the inside.

WOOD-BURNING STOVES

Wood-burning stoves come in a vast array of sizes and designs, with or without a built-in water heater. They are made of steel or cast iron. Lightweight steel is the fastest to heat up, but loses heat quickly overnight and is the least durable (performance and longevity are both improved by a brick lining). Heavy-gauge steel takes longer to warm up and cool down, costs (and weighs) more and lasts longer. Cast iron is often considered best of all, but care is needed when transporting or installing this relatively brittle and hefty material. In general, stoves are significantly more efficient than open hearths, and they can also be used for cooking. There is no denying the attraction of a 'real' fire on a winter's evening, however; if you can't live without one, consider the compromise of a Franklin stove with folding doors.

It's impossible to recommend a particular design or model of stove for all circumstances (climate, location, use, size and thermal efficiency of building), and you should seek expert advice based on your specific requirements. We have listed a selection in our Resources section on page 201.

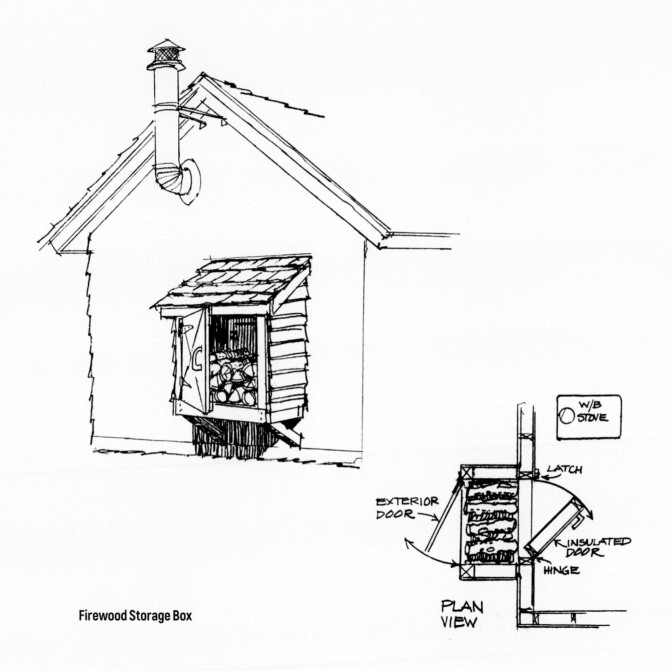

Firewood Storage Box

W/B STOVE

LATCH

EXTERIOR DOOR

INSULATED DOOR

HINGE

PLAN VIEW

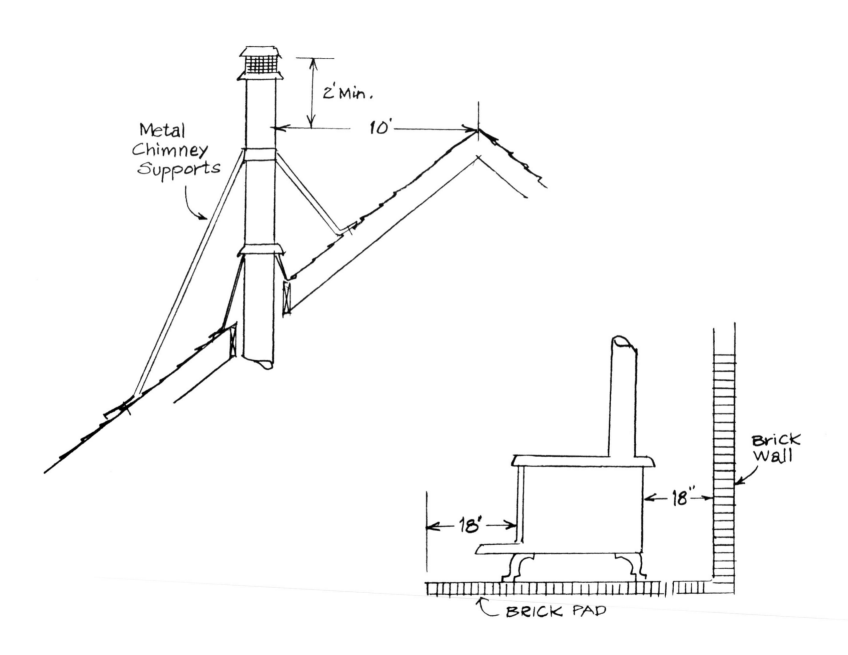

Metal Chimney Supports

2' Min.

10'

Brick Wall

18"

18'

BRICK PAD

STOVE INSTALLATION

The stove must rest on a substantial concrete, stone or brick base extending at least 18" in all directions. Keep a fire extinguisher or 5-gallon container of water nearby, and never leave a fire unattended. The wall behind the stove must be at least 3' away – unless the wall is brick or stone, or is shielded by a sheet of 28-gauge steel, in which case the minimum clearance is 18". If building any of the designs in this book, you can substitute brick for a section of the wall framing.

ELECTRIC HEATING

If your tiny house has access to an electrical supply, electric heaters are a convenient alternative. Wall-mounted models take up very little space. An on-demand water heater eliminates the need for a hot-water storage tank – saving both space and money while also reducing your carbon footprint. With an electrical connection you have the option of any modern appliance, provided it fits.

PROPANE GAS

Gas heaters may be portable, wall- or floor-mounted, or on castors. If your location makes it easy to replenish the tanks, propane is a versatile and clean option for heating and cooking; bear in mind, though, that – like kerosene – the heat it produces is wet heat and can lead to problems with condensation if the building is not adequately ventilated. Regardless of the fuel you use, it makes sense to install a carbon monoxide detector and ensure that your tiny house is not too tightly sealed against fresh air.

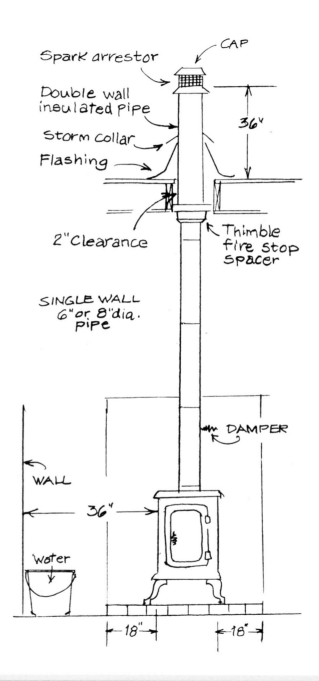

Spark arrestor
CAP
Double wall insulated pipe
Storm collar
Flashing
36"
2" Clearance
Thimble fire stop spacer
SINGLE WALL 6" or 8" dia. PIPE
DAMPER
WALL
36"
Water
18"
18"

wiring

If you have the time and want to save money, it's not hard to install electric wiring. You should start with a good DIY book on simple electric wiring *(see Resources – Books, page 202)*. Have a licensed electrician do the final hook-up, which involves setting up the service panel box and circuit breakers. The materials you need are inexpensive: under $15 (2016) for 25' of #12 Romex cable and approximately $1 each for the wall boxes. Note: The larger the wire size, the smaller the number. Use a #12 grounded cable – the third (green) wire is grounded to the box. You will also need cable clamps where the wires enter and exit the boxes, and a receptacle or switch for each box.

Leave 6" of wire on the inside of the box for connecting the receptacles and switches. The cable should be secured a maximum of 8" from the box, using special protective staples. Always install the wires before the insulation of the walls or ceiling; drill ⅝" holes through the studs with an auger bit, to run the wires. If there is any chance that a nail could be driven into the wire, protect it with a steel plate. Use a utility knife to cut a groove in the back of any rigid insulation panel, and fit the cable in the groove.

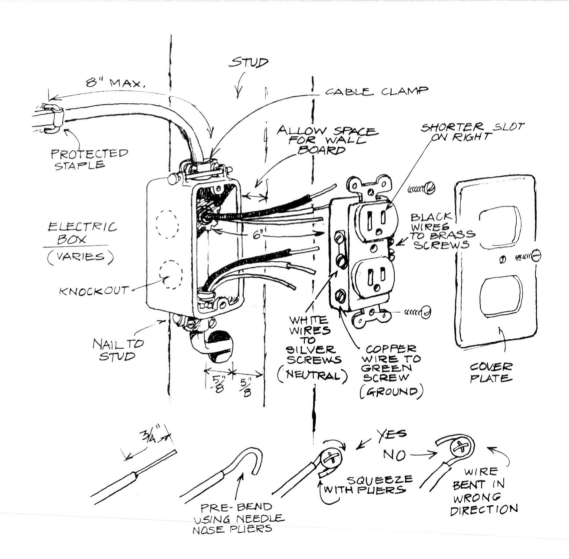

Wiring

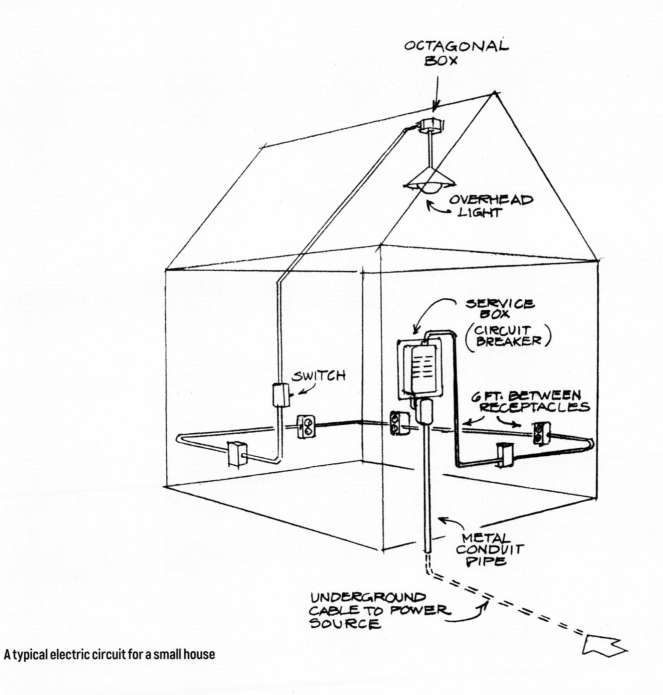

OCTAGONAL
BOX

OVERHEAD
LIGHT

SERVICE
BOX
(CIRCUIT
BREAKER)

SWITCH

6 FT. BETWEEN
RECEPTACLES

METAL
CONDUIT
PIPE

UNDERGROUND
CABLE TO POWER
SOURCE

A typical electric circuit for a small house

insulation

Centuries ago, people hung tapestries on their walls to keep out cold and drafts; those who couldn't afford them would use straw, paper and even seaweed to insulate their homes. Today, the most popular insulation in the U.S. is fiberglass wool, because it's easy to install and relatively inexpensive.

Fiberglass is environmentally friendly, has a high R value (R – 3.1 per inch), does not absorb water and is not flammable. It can irritate the eyes, lungs and skin, so take sensible precautions when handling it: wear a breathing mask, goggles, long-sleeved shirt and gloves when installing it.

In most cases fiberglass insulation is held in place by friction; however, some building codes require you to unfold and staple the paper flange on each side of the roll to the inside of the studs. If you have to cut and fit an odd piece of fiberglass insulation, cut it ½" over-size to make sure it fits snugly. Fill even the smallest spaces with a piece of torn-off insulation – any gaps may be reflected in your heating bill forever. Also, take care to place insulation behind light receptacles and plumbing pipes that could otherwise freeze and break.

To cut fiberglass insulation, place the roll on an unfinished floor, fuzzy side up; using a metal straight-edge such as a framing square, cut the roll with a utility knife.

Many other types of insulation, such as cellulose and sprayed polyurethane foam, need to be installed by professionals, which inevitably drives up the price.

Rigid insulation is a popular alternative because of its high R value. It comes in long panels of various thicknesses and is easily cut to fit using a handsaw. There are three types:

Expanded Polystyrene (EPS)
- least expensive
- white
- vapor-permeable

Extruded Polystyrene (XPS)
- crush-resistant
- blue or pink
- water-resistant

Polyisocyanurate (PIR)
- highest R Value
- foil faced
- absorbs water

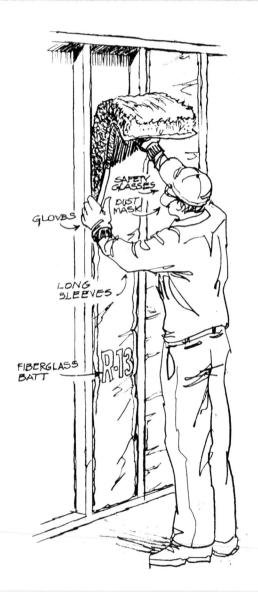

GLOVES

SAFETY GLASSES

DUST MASK!

LONG SLEEVES

FIBERGLASS BATT

R-13

We find it difficult to make a perfect fit between studs and rigid foam insulation, and always fill any cracks with foam adhesive caulking. (Make sure the caulking is compatible with your chosen insulation.) We cover the extruded polystyrene with a ⅜" coating of our own recipe for stucco: 50% Structo-Lite plaster and 50% drywall joint compound; this has held up successfully for 15 years and counting. If you try this, make sure to cover the joints with fiberglass tape before troweling on the mixture.

One the most interesting eco-friendly types of insulations is denim – literally, shredded old blue jeans. The material is reprocessed much like fiberglass into rolls and batts, and is installed the same way. If sustainability is your goal, this is a great choice. Denim insulation is a very good sound absorber and is safe to install; however it is more expensive than fiberglass. Another eco-friendly option is rockwool (also referred to as stone wool or mineral wool), also a good insulator and sound baffle *(see Resources – Insulation, page 201).*

water

Aside from oxygen, water is the most essential element for living on this planet. We all know water evaporates from oceans and lakes into the atmosphere, then falls back to earth as rain and snow; once it settles on the ground, gravity takes it to the lowest point to form rivers and lakes. Water seeps down until it reaches solid bedrock, forming aquifers, underground lakes or saturated sediment. It's amazing that fresh water aquifers are even found under the salt-water ocean.

Water is a basic necessity. We wash, drink, cook and clean with it. Unless you are lucky enough to live near an open stream or lake that has been certified safe for drinking, you may have to bring in large jugs of potable water. Various types of water jugs with convenient carrying handles are sold for this purpose (see Resources – Water, page 201).

How much drinking water should be allowed for each person? Recommendations vary, but the Mayo Clinic suggests six to eight 8-ounce glasses (1.5 to 1.9 liters) per day for healthy living. Another rule of thumb is to divide your body weight (in pounds) by two to get the number of ounces of drinking water required per day. For example, if you weigh 130 pounds, dividing by two gives you 65 ounces (eight 8-ounce glasses), the recommended amount.

If you are not sure of the quality of your drinking water, you can buy water purification tablets (as used by the military) that contain iodine. A bottle of 50 may be enough for two weeks – two tablets are used per 1 quart of water (see Resources).

Traditionally, every rural homestead had its own well and water was drawn out of the ground by bucket or hand pump. One of the first considerations when building a house was locating the water source. Quite often the well was dug first, then the house built over it, so the well pump could be located in the kitchen where it was needed. This also helped prevent the well water from freezing. A few years ago we were contracted to renovate a 1780 house that still had an outdoor well and a hand pump in the back yard. The present-day owner told us that whenever there was a power outage (typical for the end of Long Island) her neighbors would march over with buckets and fill them from her well. As a kid David often visited a farm where there was a hand pump well. As the car drove up the dirt road, it was always a race to see who could jump out first, reach the pump and start drawing water.

One option, for hardy types, is to drill (dig) your own well using a post-hole auger. Check first with local well drillers in your community to find out what type of soil your area has, and how deep you may have to drill to find water. A shallow well can be dug in a day (in ideal conditions) at the cost of a few hundred dollars. You will need an auger, such as the Seymour AU-S6, several lengths of pipe and couplings to extend the handle, and a strong back. Once the hole is dug and you reach water, you will need some plastic pipe to line the hole, and a well point at the bottom. Water will filter into the pipe through the screen of the well point. You will also need a pump – either electric or good old-fashioned hand-powered.

You can prevent contaminants from seeping to the surface of the well by casting a concrete sleeve around the pipe where the pump is attached. The water you get from the well is meant for washing or bathing, but if approved by your local water authorities it may be potable. If in doubt, boiling the water will kill any pathogens, although it will not remove chemical toxins. Many communities require that a test hole be dug before building a house. If you are lucky, you may find water 12 to 20 feet under the ground; however if your area is known for its bedrock, forget about doing it yourself!

RAINWATER CATCHMENT

Water can also be harvested from the roof of your tiny house.

To learn more about this subject we contacted Denison Stockman, who lived (and designed dozens of houses) in the Caribbean for 36 years. He said:

On most mountainous small islands of the Caribbean, there is no ground water for wells and the terrain is too steep and high to pipe water from sea level desalination plants. Houses

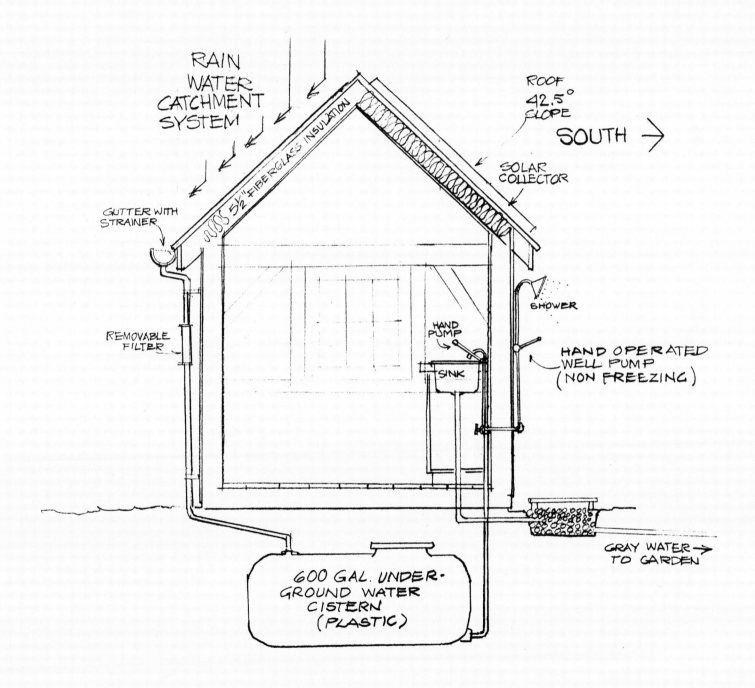

RAIN WATER CATCHMENT SYSTEM

ROOF 42.5° SLOPE

SOUTH →

5½" FIBERGLASS INSULATION

SOLAR COLLECTOR

GUTTER WITH STRAINER

SHOWER

REMOVABLE FILTER

HAND PUMP

SINK

HAND OPERATED WELL PUMP (NON FREEZING)

600 GAL. UNDER-GROUND WATER CISTERN (PLASTIC)

GRAY WATER → TO GARDEN

are constructed with storage cisterns, usually of concrete, and roofs are used to harvest rainwater. The European colonial builders historically used corrugated iron roofs, easily stacked and shipped from Europe on sailing vessels, painted with red rust-proof paint, steeply pitched to catch and channel rainwater to a gutter and downspout system, filling the cistern for later use. The corrugations also prevented collected rainfall from blowing off the roof due to squally winds during a rainstorm. Today, in the U.S. Virgin Islands, building codes require 10 gallons of cistern storage for each square foot of roof area for a single story building, 15 for two or more stories. So a 1600 square foot house would require a 16,000-gallon cistern.

Roof debris needs to be kept from washing into the cistern, so gutters need screening at the downspout outlet and need to be cleaned of leaves regularly. If the gutter isn't easily accessible from the ground, incorporate a leaf diverter at waste level in the downspout that diverts debris while allowing the water to continue into the cistern (see detail sketch above). Our roofs are normally steeply pitched and slickly finish coated, uncomfortable for birds to land and linger, but cistern water needs to be kept free of bugs, small critters and their byproducts, so overflows need to be screened as well. If the cistern is small, water purification tablets are readily available to keep water potable.

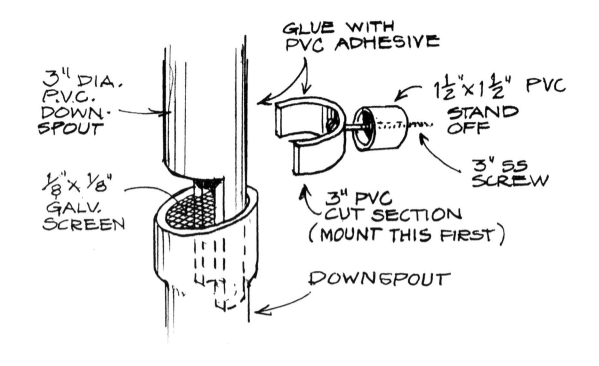

LEAF SCREEN & DOWNSPOUT DETAIL

Depending on your situation, a garden hose might be connected from a nearby source, run underground to your dwelling and mounted to a kitchen sink.

BATHING

Water is obviously necessary for bathing. If you don't have plumbing in your building, you could simply buy a plastic inflatable kiddie pool. The water can be heated on a wood burning stove. The pool is lightweight enough to drag outside for emptying. Bathing water is grey water and is excellent for irrigating a garden.

If your structure is designed for summer use only, you might consider building an outside shower from salvaged lumber. Campers and sailors have for years used a black plastic bag to heat water in the sun – in the right weather, the bag can warm up in as little as three hours. On purpose-made solar showers, a temperature gauge tells you when the water is hot enough for a comfortable shower, and there is a removable hose with showerhead. Five gallons is enough hot water for one person. For greater indulgence, install a propane gas water heater *(see Resources – Heating, page 201).*

For a more permanent solution to bathing you may want to have an enclosed bathroom in your mini-home. This would entail having a water supply for a bathroom sink and shower (unless you use the kitchen sink to brush your teeth, etc.). If you have a composting toilet, you won't need water for the toilet.

If you are building a separate room for a sink and shower, it is a good idea to water-proof the floor and walls. Fit a drain in the floor with a plastic pipe leading outside to a septic tank and leaching field. It would also be beneficial to connect the drainpipe to the kitchen sink drain. This "grey water" is good for watering your garden.

If you are planning to use this as a permanent structure, you should check regulations with your local Board of Health. Some areas don't allow composting toilets. They may require a survey of your property, a building permit and installation of a septic system. There are usually regulations regarding how far your cesspool or absorption field must be from any well. In some areas, you might be allowed to connect to an existing sanitary system, which would avoid some of the expense of hiring an excavator to dig trenches and/or install a cesspool.

toilets

The type of toilet facility you choose depends on where your tiny house is situated and how long you plan to live there. For example, if you're living in a particular place for a short time, you might rent a portable toilet, often referred to as a "Porta Potti" and have it serviced periodically; on the other hand, a permanent home will need a more elaborate septic system based on how many people are likely to live in the house. If you can't connect to existing services, you will need to obtain permits from your local Building Department and Board of Health, and hire a contractor to dig trenches for a septic tank and an absorption field or cesspool. You'll also need a source of water to carry waste through the pipes to the septic system and to clean the toilet. If the source is a well, it must be located some distance from the septic system – check your local building codes. You may also need a separate grease trap to remove "grey water" (such as soap, bathwater and food particles) from the kitchen sink. You may be able to filter grey water through the grease trap and use it to water the garden.

If codes allow, a "loveable loo" works well, especially when you are first homesteading: it is essentially a plastic 5-gallon bucket with a sealed cover, in a box that can be disguised as furniture. The design is sold commercially but is easy to make using stock lumber. Add a shovelful of sawdust (or other suitable carbon-based material) after each use, and empty into a composting bin when full – maybe once a week for one person. This is easier if there is a small exterior door in the rear of the house so the pail can be removed for composting and cleaning. Used correctly, this system is odor-free *(see Resources – Books, page 202).* There are also numerous high-tech composting commercial toilets on the market.

Other off-grid toilets have a built-in water reservoir and hand-operated spray jets to clean the bowl, or incinerators using electricity or propane gas that burn waste to ashes.

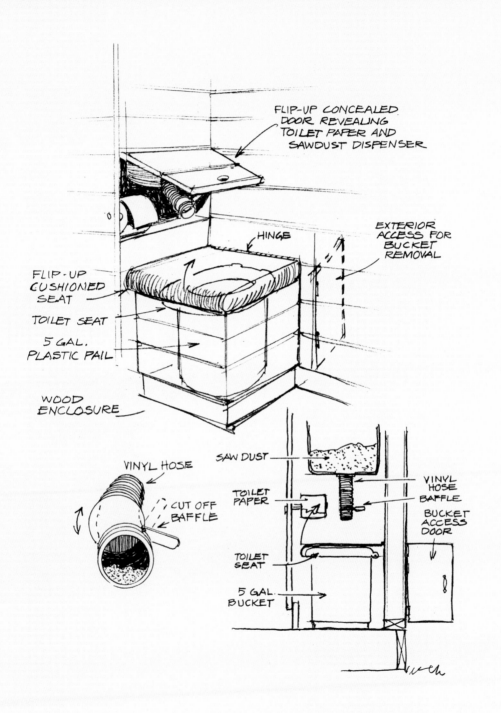

FLIP-UP CONCEALED
DOOR REVEALING
TOILET PAPER AND
SAWDUST DISPENSER

EXTERIOR
ACCESS FOR
BUCKET
REMOVAL

HINGE

FLIP-UP
CUSHIONED
SEAT

TOILET SEAT

5 GAL.
PLASTIC PAIL

WOOD
ENCLOSURE

VINYL HOSE

CUT OFF
BAFFLE

SAW DUST

VINYL
HOSE
BAFFLE

TOILET
PAPER

BUCKET
ACCESS
DOOR

TOILET
SEAT

5 GAL.
BUCKET

kitchen planning

For many people, the kitchen is the most important room – the heart of the house. How can you have a proper kitchen in a tiny house, or invite friends to dinner?

If you are considering downsizing to a tiny house but are worried how you would cook and entertain, read the advice given by Carolyn Shearlock (www.theboatgalley.com), who has lived on a sailboat for several years. Her tips on how to provision in a small space are just as pertinent to a tiny house. For example, she discovered a compact cooking pot that can cook a delicious meal for six people. It is often possible to buy small versions of appliances (such as gas or electric refrigerators) designed for marine or camping use.

A wood-burning stove can save space by doubling as heat source and burners; it can also heat water at the same time. For baking, an accessory metal box can be used on top of the stove *(see Resources – Heating, page 201)*. The early settlers had "summer kitchens." When it became too hot indoors, they just moved the cooking outside under a covered roof.

If you are off-grid, it can be hard to keep food such as milk and butter from spoiling. Our early settlers built "spring houses" partially sunk in the ground or sometimes over streams. In some cases deep wells were used to store food where the mean earth temperature remains fairly constant. The temperature is said to remain about 50°-55° at a depth of 4' in most areas of the United States.

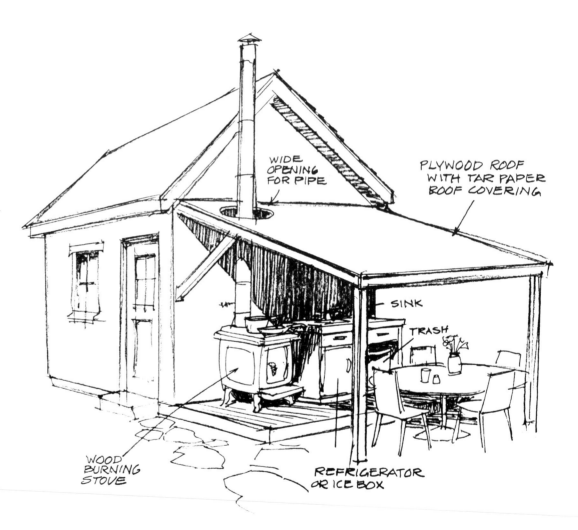

WIDE OPENING FOR PIPE

PLYWOOD ROOF WITH TAR PAPER ROOF COVERING

SINK

TRASH

WOOD BURNING STOVE

REFRIGERATOR OR ICE BOX

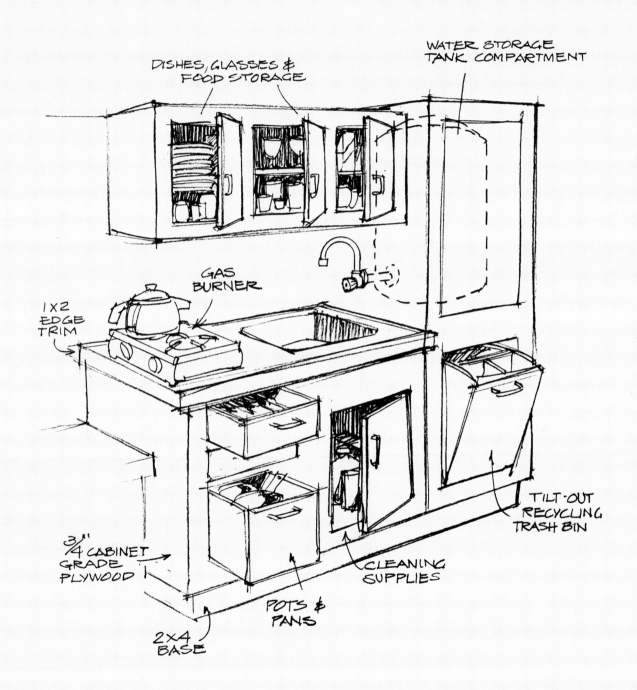

DISHES, GLASSES &
FOOD STORAGE

WATER STORAGE
TANK COMPARTMENT

GAS
BURNER

1X2
EDGE
TRIM

3/4" CABINET
GRADE
PLYWOOD

2X4
BASE

POTS &
PANS

CLEANING
SUPPLIES

TILT-OUT
RECYCLING
TRASH BIN

Less than a century ago, large ice blocks were cut out of freshwater lakes in winter, and shipped to cities for storage in deep icehouses insulated with sawdust or straw. Before modern refrigeration, homes relied on ice delivered regularly and stored in real iceboxes; as the ice slowly melted, the homeowner would have to empty the drip pan underneath. Ice blocks and dry ice are still available in some cities and are often bought by football fans for "tailgate parties," or by campers who need ice for just a few days and store it in Styrofoam coolers.

Propane gas refrigerators are an option in the absence of electricity. They are more expensive than electric refrigerators, and less widely available. Make sure to use a licensed plumber for the installation. Electric refrigerators offer the widest range of types, generally using regular household current. Small, inexpensive, dormitory-type refrigerators will fit most tiny houses. Refrigerators that use DC current are also available for solar installations that don't have inverters to change to AC current.

The compact size of mini-kitchens makes them ideal for a tiny house. Most units contain a sink and faucet, a two-burner stove, storage and a refrigerator.

The kitchen has a counter with a sink. The water is stored in a tank in the upper corner cabinet; "grey water" drains into a drywell outside, or you can use it to water a garden. If the garden is located downhill, this is an especially practical solution. The kitchen cabinet base has two storage drawers and shelves for pots and pans. Above the counter is a cabinet convenient for dishes and dry food storage.

Factory-build mini-kitchens are also available. Most units contain a sink and faucet, a two-burner stove, storage compartment and refrigerator *(see Resources – Mini Kitchens, page 201).*

space-saving solutions

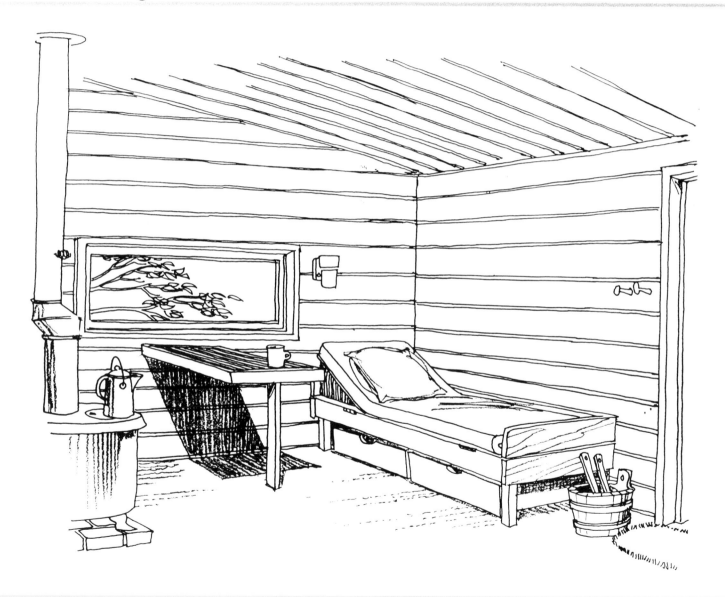

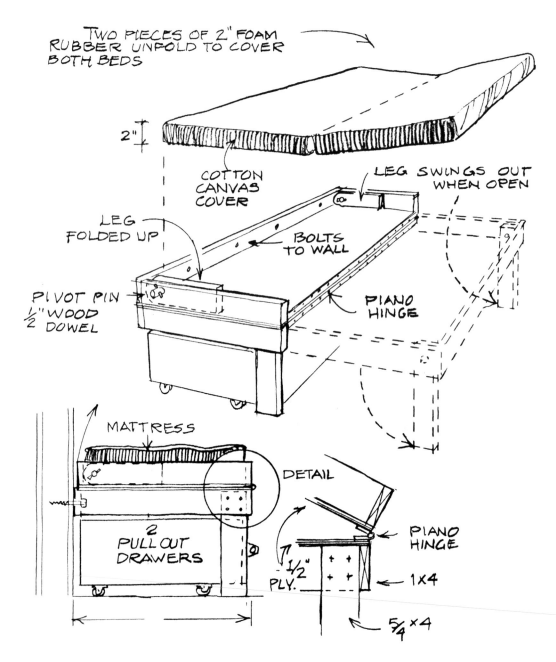

TWO PIECES OF 2" FOAM RUBBER UNFOLD TO COVER BOTH BEDS

2"

COTTON CANVAS COVER

LEG FOLDED UP

LEG SWINGS OUT WHEN OPEN

BOLTS TO WALL

PIVOT PIN 1/2" WOOD DOWEL

PIANO HINGE

MATTRESS

2 PULL OUT DRAWERS

DETAIL

PIANO HINGE

1/2" PLY.

1×4

5/4 × 4

FOLD-OUT BED

A couch folds out into a double bed covered with a 3" thick foam mattress. Two storage bins (one at each end) hold extra blankets and towels. We built and used this fold-out bed in our cabin and it worked perfectly. Under the bed are two pullout drawers for storing clothes.

FOLD-DOWN TABLE

This table serves as a writing or eating table. We placed ours at the window to enjoy the view. It folds down to allow room for the double bed.

DOOR FILE STORAGE

Storing files and papers can be a problem if you live in a small dwelling or apartment. David's small studio began to overflow with stacks of files containing manuscript copies of the 24 books we have written, plus his original illustrations.

It suddenly dawned on us that we were overlooking valuable storage space on the back of our office closet door. As you can see from the picture, we built four file storage boxes out of ½" birch plywood and placed them out of sight until needed.

This is an easy project for anybody with a table saw at their disposal, or who can get the lumberyard to make the cuts (see Cutting Plan on page 150). The width of the back is based on a 24"-wide panel door. Adjust plans if necessary. It would only take half a day to make and fifteen minutes to mount on the door. It's all made from half a sheet of ½" plywood, fast-setting wood glue and 1¼" steel brads.

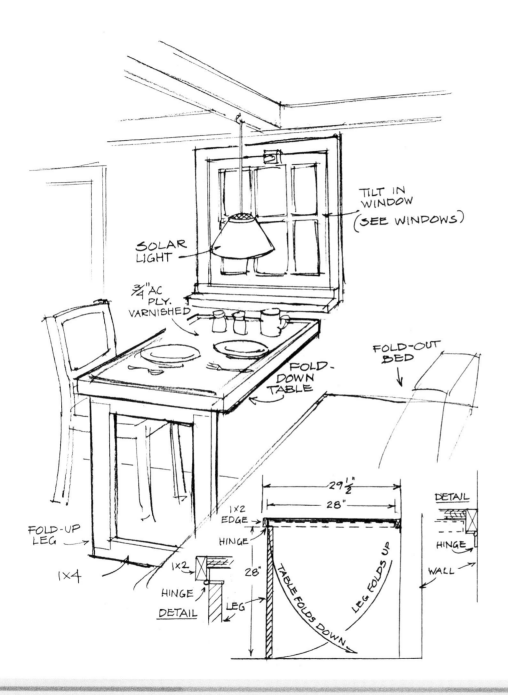

TILT IN
WINDOW
(SEE WINDOWS)

SOLAR
LIGHT

¾" AC
PLY.
VARNISHED

FOLD-
DOWN
TABLE

FOLD-OUT
BED

FOLD-UP
LEG

1×4

1×2
EDGE

HINGE

1×2

HINGE

DETAIL

LEG

DETAIL

HINGE

WALL

29½"

28"

28"

TABLE FOLDS DOWN

LEG FOLDS UP

Once the pieces are cut out, the easiest way to assemble them is to glue the pieces together and then hammer in the brads before the glue has fully set. For a first-rate job, sand off the sharp edges and smooth the surfaces using a palm-sander with #220-grit sandpaper.

Mount the boxes on the closet door by first drilling four ⅛" pilot holes in the back of each box, and screw them to the door using 1¼"-long, round-head screws.

Since the screws will show, you may want to use finishing washers around them for a truly professional look.

SLANTED BASE

The base of the box is slanted to progressively raise the files so that the labels can be easily read. This step is not necessary if you don't intend to use it for files.

Start with a piece of ½" plywood measuring 3½" x 12½". Set your table saw-blade to a 70° bevel. Cut a bevel on one long side of the plywood. Turn the board over and cut a bevel on the opposite side. Test for fit and trim as necessary.

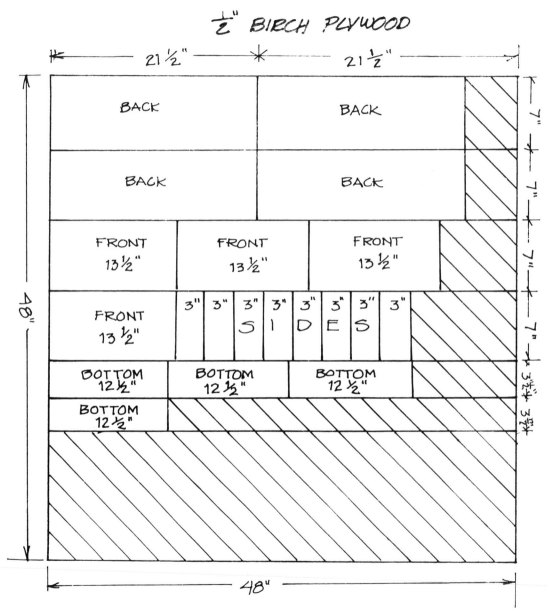

Door File Storage Cutting Plan

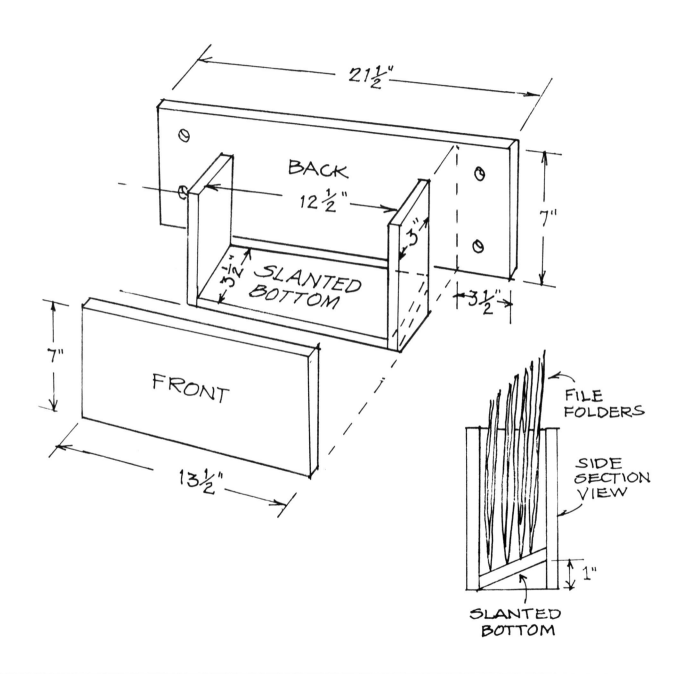

21½"

BACK

12½"

7"

3"

3½"

3½"

SLANTED BOTTOM

7"

FRONT

13½"

FILE FOLDERS

SIDE SECTION VIEW

1"

SLANTED BOTTOM

THREE | living small success stories

There's nothing new about living small: the Greek philosopher Diogenes famously lived in a "barrel" (actually a large clay jar), and through the ages many saints, hermits and other colorful characters have been associated with caves and remote cottages; but today it doesn't have to be about privation or isolation. People from all walks of life are drawn to the idea of a simpler, less cluttered existence. We asked several notable bloggers and tiny house enthusiasts for their own insights and views. This is what they said...

crooked river tiny house – lon cameron

living small: a road trip across america

BY DAKOTA ARKIN CAFOUREK

My possessions have seldom filled more than three rooms. I have been an urbanite for the better part of my adult life, and city living has made existing in small spaces familiar. We brush through empty pockets in crowded sidewalks to pass amblers, find our own stillness on a crowded subway and make eye contact with the bartender like there isn't a room full of others doing the same. We live stacked atop and alongside the other inhabitants of our city and are suspicious of quiet. Our way of life is a doorstep to experiencing the excitement outside – an anonymous expedition through the city's stage. I have often considered my apartments a mere personal credenza in the likes of New York City, Paris and Berlin. And like the real estate adage, the smaller the apartment, the more grandiose the experience outside: location, location, location. It also meant: expensive.

And so, when my fiancé, Andrew, and I made the transition from a one-bedroom garden apartment in Cobble Hill to a car, the move was driven by the promise of grandiosity beyond our Brooklyn dwelling – one that would swell to the whole of the United States.

In a perfect storm of rising rents, West Coast wedding invitations and new career hopes, I quit my job. We packed our belongings into a 10' x 10' storage unit in Quogue and transformed our Buick Encore, a compact SUV, into our kitchen, dining, den and bedroom-on-the-go. It would be the smallest quarters we'd ever had, but environs as dreamy as the Colorado Rockies, the canyons of Wyoming, the Pacific Coast Highway and beyond would become our front porch, our back deck and long driveway.

In a few short days, our clothes, toiletries, camping mugs, first-aid kits, USB cords and HDMI cables filled my childhood bedroom in Amagansett, New York. From one village west of Montauk ("The End" of Long Island), Andrew and I prepared for everything we thought we might need to cross the country from the easternmost part of New York to the coast of California. I was energized in a whirlwind of imagination, and my native Minnesotan, outdoor aficionado fiancé guided our way. I recall the night before leaving, Andrew looked at our first-aid kit and then at me. "You know what to do if we're hiking, I fall on a rock and start bleeding profusely, right?" "Nope, no idea," I responded with assurance, confident in my inexperience. He sighed. The minutiae of organization removed our minds from feared unknowns awaiting us in our big adventure. In a small space, we knew that thoughtful organization would be paramount and so we reclaimed six stackable plastic drawers left over from my college dorm room, and grabbed two taller, narrower sets of plastic drawers at a nearby store. Like the New York skyscrapers we were leaving behind, our belongings would be tall and stacked.

We each took three of the drawers, using them as our own clothing bins. I brought everything from water-resistant bike pants to a pair of stilettos. Andrew packed arguably less, but a tie made it in the mix for the three weddings we would be attending. We packed jogging gear, camping gear, a range of clothes fit for brunch in San Francisco, ATV riding in Montana and a spirit tasting in Nashville. "Neither snow, nor rain, nor heat…" would be dodged. I dedicated one drawer to socks, undergarments, a scarf, hat, gloves and a bathing suit. One drawer carried my outdoorsy gear, from jeans to tees and tanks to running tights. My remaining drawer

included dress pants, blouses, a fancy dress and a sundress. Andrew, minus the dresses, added a bottle of whiskey to keep us warm over the campfire.

We removed the back seats of the car, which added significantly to the space and helped keep a level foundation for our packed items. Our clothing drawers would be accessible through the rear hatch of the car. This later drew strange looks from passers-by, as it was not infrequently we were parked on a sidewalk in Nashville or Portland, grabbing a new pair of socks or a change of clothes from the back dressers in our vehicle.

The two remaining stackable bins were our kitchenette, our toiletries drawer, even our junk drawer for maps and other tiny souvenirs we acquired along the way. In it, we also carried Andrew's embossed National Park Passport, which we would stamp at the various parks visited on our journey – from the Great Smoky Mountains to Yellowstone National Park. We each kept a toiletries bag, shared a giant bottle of Dr. Bronner's Almond Soap (which also came in handy for washing dishes) plus I had packed a makeup bag, blow dryer, comb and brush. These bins were accessible from the driver's side rear door or with a long backward stretch between the front seats of the vehicle. In the drawer most accessible from the passenger seat, we kept our on-the-go pantry - full of crackers, raw almonds, and occasionally gummies and licorice.

The rest of our kitchenette drawers contained camping plates, mugs and bowls, silverware, a chef's knife, a mandolin - not for playing, but for julienned bell peppers – and a cutting board. On the road ahead, the actual places we would lay our head would

What gave you the idea?

I impulsively bought a 3.5 acre lot on the Crooked River and knew I wanted to build something but assumed I had to pay a lot and get contractors involved and prepare myself for a hefty mortgage, etc. Once I realized the actual costs associated with a big construction project, reality hit and I knew I needed to look for an alternative. I visited some friends in central Maine who were living in a shed while they saved to build their house, and I fell in love with the shed concept. I started looking around online, stumbled upon the tiny house blog, and went from there.

Did you build it yourself?

Yes. My brother helped to excavate the lot and carve the driveway. The only thing I've subcontracted was the installation of 9 pre-cast concrete piers in November 2009 ($2500). Everything else I built myself.

Did you have previous building experience?

No. I attended a 2-day building workshop offered by Vermont Tiny Houses (Peter King). It taught me to use the tools necessary to do the work, and to learn the basic math and foresight involved with framing a tiny house.

Did you design it yourself?

Yes. I actually was staying in a large apartment as part of a housesitting gig over someone's garage in Cape Elizabeth and I used the floor space to tape out my floor plan (10x14) using masking tape and measurements I'd taken from the door and windows, couch, and cabinets that I purchased via Craigslist and Habitat Restores… I bought those items before I built the house, and then designed the house

around them. (In hindsight, I'm glad I did it this way as it's much cheaper to build something around the more expensive aspects – like doors and windows – than to build something and pay even more for a custom fit.)

Did the plans or design evolve as you went along?

The layout I designed after I purchased my door and windows, as aforementioned. The overall design definitely has taken its own evolution over time; I wasn't sure what I would have for a ladder, where to put a cooktop, what kind of flooring, how everything would fit together.

How long did it take to build; and were you working full-time or weekends/holidays?

One full year of most weekends to get to an insulated, sealed structure (and that's with using hammer and nails). The guest house/composting toilet building was sealed in two weekends using a generator with pneumatic tools – significantly faster.

Did anyone help build?

Friends have come out and helped with small parts here and there, but really it's mostly been just myself.

Were you able to use power tools?

I built the house itself using a $200 Craftsmen combo rechargeable battery-powered tool kit. I still use the tools, and I have since expanded the line to include several rechargeable battery-operated lights for use at the house… and a radio for the wild dance parties, of course.

range from campsites to AirBnBs, hotels to guest bedrooms. Cooking would be a way to show gratitude to many of our hosts and ensure economic and healthy choices sans kitchen. Accessible from the passenger rear door was our Coleman Powerchill 40 Quart Thermoelectric Chiller. It charged in the standard plug built into the center console of the car and kept at a steady 40° F below the outside temperature while using less energy than a mini-refrigerator. In this way, we could pull over on the Blue Ridge Parkway, grab cheese and prosciutto out of our chiller, slice up a tomato and construct a sandwich for consuming at a serene, empty picnic table with a vista of North Carolina. We did not consume fast food a single time on our travels through 29 states over six months.

Storage bags from the IKEA Skubb collection and a handful of vacuum bags made by Ziploc also proved imperative to our packing. Large bags were handy for storing vacuum-sealed winter wear that we would not need for several months of West Coast living. Small bags were great for shoes – from my hiking boots to flip flops, sneakers, stilettos and ankle boots. Needless to say, I brought along more pairs of shoes than Andrew. An array of camping gear slipped into the car like real life Tetris.

From campsites to weddings in wine country and the many cities and sites in-between, we were as prepared as we could be. Our own country had been such uncharted territory for me. Our car was now packed and, ready or not, the journey was starting now. A not-to-scale New York state magnet was affixed to the rear of our car, with 47 others ready in waiting: Alaska and Hawaii were unlikely destinations this trip. A GoPro hitched to our front dashboard was set to record the drive at 60-second intervals (which we eventually improved to capture every 30 seconds) and on a sun-filled late August morning we faced the car toward Indian Wells Beach in Amagansett and hit Record. The sand looked especially white and the ocean a most vibrant blue as the sun brightened and emboldened the beach. The adventure was underway. Living small would be our roadmap to living large.

Our tour of the U.S. would take us southward through Washington, D.C., North Carolina and Tennessee. We would then venture west into Arkansas, north through Missouri and up into South Dakota. Westbound, we'd cross the badlands into Wyoming, Montana and ultimately reach San Francisco. From Seattle to San Diego, Andrew and I covered the coast before our eastward return across The Loneliest Road in America through Nevada into Utah. 2,330 miles from Amagansett, we took an impromptu route through Colorado, visiting Aspen, Telluride and Ouray before heading south on the Million Dollar Highway to Santa Fe. Eastbound once again, we high-tailed across Texas to Southwest Missouri for the holidays, followed by a frigid January visit to Columbus, Ohio and ultimately a rush to beat the most epic snowstorm of 2016 to reach New York City – where the city welcomed us back with a miracle parking space right outside the apartment, and then held us captive for two days of snowfall.

As much as we were prepared, there were still a number of unforeseen improvements we would make along the way. A week into our trip, we spent our first night in the outdoors at the Honeybear Campground in Boone, North

Cost to build?
Around $7500… including the foundation/pier installation.

What are the dimensions of your building?
10' x 14' with 8' x 10' loft; 2x6 walls, 2x8 rafters.

It's insulated, so is it usable in the winter?
Yes! Very much so. I used cotton denim insulation (http://bit.ly/2mELGh4). I just tore it by hand and stuffed it accordingly.

(But it was a higher R-value, like 30.) Then I wrapped and taped the entire interior with double bubble foil insulation (http://bit.ly/2mKIWOh).

What about heating & cooking?
My wood-burning stove is a Jotul 602 – double-walled black pipe. What's nice is I found a pop-in screen for viewing the fire or to tone it down a little bit. The door easily pulls off, and the screen pops in (http://bit.ly/2lcai3F).

For cooking I use a Suburban 3-burner drop-in propane cooktop (http://bit.ly/2lcbofK).

Water source?
Drinking water is brought in by hand.

For the shower, a 5-gallon bucket is used to retrieve water from the river for dishes, bathing, etc. I put a hand spray shower head and a plastic tank sprayer together to make the shower unit: (http://low.es/2mF8tJp and http://low.es/2lWvZSu).

I painted the spray container black, so in the summer, the water heats up nicely from the sun. Otherwise, a big pot is heated over the cooktop and then poured into the container. Makes for about a 5-minute shower. The on/off switch on the head is key so you can shut the water off while you pump to build pressure.

For dish washing, I have a sink basin in the house for draining water, which is hooked up to a grey-water treatment system; Maine lists these as approved grey-water treatment (http://bit.ly/2mdhZWM). It was a lot of hand digging, but I'm happy with the result and it was user-friendly to install for someone who had zero plumbing experience!

Composting toilet?
For my toilet setup I use a urine diversion kit from http://www.abetterwaytogo.com.au. Essentially there is a 5-gallon bucket for collecting solids, and a separate 5-gallon bucket for collecting urine. The urine bucket just gets tossed into the woods every couple of days; occasionally I'll add river water and use it for plants. The solids are rotated out; there are 12 buckets with these

Carolina. We set up our tent, yoga mats, plaid wool blanket and lanterns; we even a brought a bistro-style table and entry rug for more of a "glamping" feel. The temperatures dropped into the low 40s and our plan to sleep on sheets and use one sleeping bag as a duvet proved a total failure. The next day, we made a visit to R.E.I. and purchased an additional sleeping bag – there is a science to staying warm and we opted in. Our next camping edition was in North-eastern Arkansas where temperatures and humidity levels surpassed 90° F and 90 percent, and we were awake by dawn for the sheer joy of returning to air conditioning.

It was also on these camping experiments where we learned that while our car was expertly packed, it was not easily unpackable. We soon purchased a 20 cu. ft. X-Cargo topper from Sears and our new attic would hold our lanterns, tents, sleeping bags and all the rest of our camping equipment which made the entire set-up and takedown process easier by two-fold. As winter approached a few months later near Lake Tahoe, we also learned about California's requirement for snow chains and purchased a pair of these to have ready for our tires. In Aspen, a blizzard hit and I purchased a pair of ski pants and a ski jacket at a nearby thrift shop as I realized my original plan of layers was not going to cut it. It also suited me for an impromptu day on the slopes while Andrew found a company called Suit Yourself, where a guy named Lorenzo showed up in a parking lot with a van full of ski and snowboard gear of all kinds and sizes, and on the mountain we were.

For us, the practicalities of living and working on the road are dependent on Internet access. Monday thru Friday lose their meaning

screw-on lids total (http://amzn.to/2lceEI0). When a bucket is about ½ full, it's removed from the back hatch of the privy system, the lid is screwed on, and then it is placed in the available opening of the bucket composting box; the next bucket in the lineup is then taken out. The contents are semi-composted down already, and the contents are then dumped into one of the larger bins seen behind it. Now that empty bucket is placed into the privy to be used again. With rotating buckets for a full year, the composter is only about ⅓ full. Essentially, once one composter is ½ to ¾ full, I'm going to leave that one to just sit and collect occasional handfuls of leaves, and the other composter will then begin collecting the solids. Once the second composter is ½ to ¾ full, I'll remove the contents of the first composter and spread it around the woods or bury it or use it on perennial beds. I've been using this system for about 4 years now and love it: it's low-key, not odorous, easy maintenance and was cheap to set up over time. I've added a new element to the design each year. The first year, I just rotated a couple of buckets, the next year I built the black box, the next year I added more buckets and larger composters, and this year I built a roof over the system so snow won't collapse any of it and it will be accessible year-round. So, what is there is not holistically low-budget the way I have it set up (~$500), but I only paid for the urine diverting seat setup and that kept the budget low to start for the first two years while I figured and saved for the expansion.

Electric? Solar/wind power?
I hope to incorporate solar in the next year or two.

Do you live there most of the time, or only part of?
I currently live there for 3-7 days each month while I'm in graduate school. I hope to reside there once I graduate so I can tackle my treehouse screen house vision and complete some of the landscaping projects I'd like to do around the yard while I study for my exams. Long-term, I'm unsure of where I'll be working. I would love to live here full time, but employment will ultimately dictate if it's a geographic option. If not, I'll start fresh and build small somewhere else!

What type of person uses your cabin – why do they like it? Do you have a visitors' book; if so, what comments do people make, and do you have a favorite quote?
The type of person who rents my cabin (on airbnb) wants a rustic retreat that's a step above pitching a tent, is totally unplugged from busy life stuff, and is affordable while exacting a small investment from guests. People that stay are required to bring their own drinking water, provide their own linens or sleeping bags, and to leave the place nicer than they find it. Setting these rules has helped to attract the type of guest I want to host, and so far (knock on wood), it's worked out very well. I keep a logbook at the house and have guests sign it before they check out. It's my favorite "go to" aspect of hosting and sharing my space, as I get to read about people's experiences staying at the house

to daily work sessions squeezed into the morning, afternoon or night at a café, bar or rented apartment with our laptops. It just so happened that Andrew needed to meet a deadline at the time we were camping beneath Mount Rushmore, and made multiple late night drives in pouring rain to catch one bar of phone service to push it out. For times like this we were flexible to adjust course. There was a 48-hour stop in Rapid City, SD where we barely left our hotel room diving into work, but when we lifted our heads up it was to look out onto the Badlands. For us, it was hardly a sacrifice, for we were grateful for the opportunity, even if some moments proved difficult or raised a feeling of homesickness. We tried to create a sense of stability, even amidst constantly changing locations, by limiting consecutive days on the road. This allowed us time to balance work and sightseeing. There would be weeks when we were completely motionless and committed to one city and other instances when we paused for just a night or two in a destination, propelling our way forward.

Before our first foray into the great West from Kansas City, we had seldom ever driven a distance longer than five or six hours but the sheer vastness of country beyond the Missouri River meant longer driving days and an audible "Woah!" from Andrew and me as we crossed epic canyons and valleys. The West is a place where the terrain is omnipresent and man is master of none, even dwarfing city skyscrapers as though it could swallow Manhattan in one large gulp.

The only fixed itinerary items were three weddings and the holidays. Otherwise, we determined our general destination by drawing a line on our atlas, and would start to plot

and see their artistic drawings, recipes, etc.
It's really shaped a whole Crooked River Tiny
House family of sorts. I think I would easily
be friends with many of the folks who stay. It's
been very rewarding to have other people enjoy
being there as much as my dog (Max) and I.

*After years of hopping from one long-term hous-
esitting gig to another, Lon Cameron decided to
make a more stable home and creative space for
himself. He found some property on Craigslist
and built himself a tiny (affordable) house filled
with Goodwill finds and Habitat for Humanity
Restore deals. In 2014 he was accepted into a
masters program at UNE to become a Physi-
cian Assistant, and, because of his tight student
budget, decided to open the Crooked River Tiny
House to airbnb guests.*

*After his graduation in 2016, he was offered
a job that pulled him from the area, and so
decided to see if anyone would be interested
in purchasing the property. Keith Tiszenkel,
a former Crooked River Tiny House guest,
immediately took notice and went on to buy the
house; the two have stayed in touch, and Lon is
currently helping Keith complete a lofted screen
house close to the tiny house for him and his
guests to enjoy! The house now has an enthusiastic following of its own.*

https://www.facebook.com/crookedrivertinyhouse/
https://www.airbnb.com/rooms/14339452?guests=
1&s=8w3djW8F
Instagram@crookedrivertinyhouse

where exactly we would sleep and shower about two or three weeks ahead – I promise we had the opportunity to shower (almost) daily.

Writing this nearly a year since we set off, I can tell you we have not yet chosen a place to stay put. We've slowed down, spending more time with family on Long Island, in New York City, Columbus, Springfield, MO and Minnesota, preparing for our nuptials in the fall. Our road trip across the country began with so many unknowns and now fills our minds with memories, stories, imagery, newfound friends and experiences. It is familiar and a mark on who we are and who we will become. I learned if we can dream it, we can do it. We are still compelled to wander through cultures and landscapes, to chance upon the traditions left to us from an earlier time and the makings of this generation, and so we have not unpacked our bags. Indeed, one day in the not too distant future, we dream of seeing our furniture again, making a home for ourselves – one without wheels. Then, we will unpack.

Dakota Arkin Cafourek is a writer and editor based in New York. Her work has appeared in And North, Upward Magazine and Whalebone. She is devoted to travel, cultural immersion and the study of languages. With a background in branding and marketing, and passion for editorial, she collaborates with various brands and cultural institutions. Dakota's own adventures are chronicled on her blog, Maidstone Buttermilk. She holds a M.A. from The American University of Paris and a B.F.A. from New York University's Tisch School of the Arts.

Plenty of hooks and pegs make for great small-space storage solutions.

Even the seating at the Crooked River Tiny House allows for extra storage.

Two additional structures on the Crooked River property include a screened-in deck with additional storage underneath and a guest house and bathroom with separate entrances.

sauna hut – françois dallegret

I have had Canadian electric saunas for the past fifty years, starting at home in Westmount, then at our farm in Ways Mills and finally in Sandy Cove, Nova Scotia where we go every summer. A friend of mine originally had one, then I got the bug and built mine with a window in the basement of our house – and every three days I profit from this exciting amenity and feel great and relaxed.

In the country the tradition in the winter is to roll out in the snow and scare the passers-by.

In Nova Scotia I built a sauna hut in 2011 not far from our main cabin. It has a small bathroom, a chemical toilet, a shower outside, and a room for entertaining as well as a sleeping area upstairs. During the month of August in Sandy Cove I jump into the heat and look out at the wild surroundings, taking a very cold shower outside every 15 minutes and half-expecting to encounter a particular bear known to hang out in the same woods.

But – it is not a sauna if you don't pour a bit of your favorite beer to boil on the rocks. Being short-sighted, I can say that it is crucial to be totally naked, boys and girls, when lounging on the hot cedar benches... and not to say anything, since silence is part of the game.

Born south, François Dallegret went north where he thrives. He was trained as an architect at the École des Beaux-Arts in Paris. www.arteria.ca

François' sauna hut shown in relation to his main cabin.

I had been interested in tiny houses for several years, as part of the ethos of living more simply and with a lighter human footprint on the planet. So, I would indulge my tiny-house living fantasies by going onto websites advertising tiny houses. When I received a little money from a legal settlement, my fantasy became a little more solid: I saw the cabin (a "demo model" for Jamaica Cottages in Jamaica, Vermont) listed on tinyhomes.com and said, "That's the one for me." The cottage was $45,000, including the rural 1.3 acres it sits on. It isn't my main dwelling, but a place I can retreat to and a backup place to live as we face more turbulent times ahead in the world.

The cabin measures 14' x 20' – 240 sq. ft. without the exterior screened-in porch. It's well insulated, with a tiny but effective wood stove, a propane heater in the bedroom and a propane kitchen range. Quite toasty in the winter! The wood-burning stove is old and leaky; I plan to upgrade to a better one. Water is hauled in bottles. There's an Envirolet toilet. The cabin has electric power. It's currently a vacation cabin; people love it.

Francesca Rheannon is the producer and host of Writer's Voice. A life-long bibliophile, reading is her favorite thing to do and books are her preferred décor. http://www.writersvoice.net

heart of it all house – trevor gay & mary benasutti

What gave you the idea?

In 2011, I saw a Facebook post with one of Jay Schafer's original tiny houses. I read the benefits of downsizing and living tiny – I've been sold on the idea ever since.

Did you build it yourself?

We built our house with the help of family and a few awesome friends.

Did you have previous building experience?

I've had various building projects that were non-home related, but my father has had a handful of different building projects.

Did you design it yourself?

We bought the "hOMe" plans from TinyHouseBuild. The design and layout captured our heart; it's absolutely stunning. It works great for us.

Did the design evolve as you went along?

We slightly modified the plans but mostly just styled the house to our taste. The plans were great from the start.

How long did it take to build? Were you working full-time or weekends/holidays?

We started the build in December of 2014 and finished in May of 2015. Six months of nights and weekends as much as we possibly could!

Did anyone help build?

Trevor's mom and dad helped on the build almost everyday and let us build the house inside their barn. Mary's family and some of our close friends came and helped build as often as they could.

Were you able to use power tools?
Thankfully, we used many power tools!

How much did it cost to build?
The Heart Of It All House cost just over $33,000 to build ourselves.

What are the dimensions of your building?
28' x 8'6" x 13'6"

Is it insulated, and usable in the winter?
We used spay foam insulation in the walls and rigid foam insulation in the sub-floor. We've been through sub-zero temperatures in the house and it stays comfortable!

Heating & cooking?
We use an LG Ductless mini-split heat/ac system; we also use a supplemental small infrared heater during the extreme cold times. We have a full-size gas range stove for cooking.

Water source?
Our drinking water and shower come from the well that's on our property. We have an in-line propane on-demand water heater for the shower as well.

We chose to save space in the kitchen by excluding a dishwasher, and simply wash our dishes by hand.

Composting toilets?
We use a Separett Villa waterless composting toilet.

Electric? Solar/wind power?
Our electric is on-site 50amp service.

Do you live there most of the time or part of?
We live in our tiny house full-time.

We have a standing-seam metal roof. The exterior is cedar lap siding with a treatment we applied called "Shou Sugi Ban." This is an ancient Japanese technique used to keep away bugs and extend the life of the wood.

We have four cats in the house and have built special features such as a rope bridge, extended windowsills and an integrated scratching post for the cats.

Our kitchen features full-size appliances and a microwave with a vent fan.

Trevor Gay is a self-confessed vegan bicycle junkie born and raised in the corn fields of Ohio. Mary Benasutti is an Airforce Vet with new sites set on finishing college to help animals of all kinds. Follow their tiny house adventures at:

www.heartofitallhouse.com
Instagram@heartofitallhouse
Facebook.com/heartofitallhouse

brookside cottage – christopher stoney

One hears a lot these days about people trying to fulfill their dream of a small, sensible and affordable home, only to be frustrated by high land prices and restrictive zoning. I was lucky. I had the opportunity to purchase a small cottage essentially unchanged since the 1940s, when smaller houses were the norm.

I have always had an idea of just what kind of house I wanted to live in. For years I had been keeping an eye on the market for the perfect house. Finally, in 2006, I saw an ad in a real estate flyer: 'Brookside cottage with claw foot tub.' This I had to check out, even though I was in a perfectly comfortable living situation at the time. When I visited the house, I felt a sense of recognition. It was as if I were returning to a home I had built for myself in a previous life. In a flurry of negotiations I got the price down to what I could afford, and with the help and advice of a Tarot reader, overcame some legal hurdles to become a homeowner.

Since then, I have been redecorating/ remodeling the house one room at a time. The claw foot tub is still there, although the rest of the bathroom has been completely redone. The original uneven and treacherous 20" wide stairway has been retreaded with triangular steps, the best solution I could come up with for a space too steep for normal stairs but not steep enough for a ladder. I replaced the living-room ceiling, fitting panels cut from turquoise-painted T1-11 plywood between the joists.

The house is 16' x 24'. Except for the bath and a tiny laundry room (with its own exterior access near the clothesline), the downstairs is one open space. There is a kitchen alcove separated by an angled

One comforting thing about a small house, especially for a claustrophobe like me, is being able to see outside in all directions. A larger house would actually feel more confining, with windows on only one or two sides of each room. I like to think of my house as a garment that I hold around myself for warmth and comfort as I look out into the world that is my home. I think of myself as living not in a house, but in a place: a wooded glade by a brook, in a neighborhood of good friends, in a college town with an abundance of cultural activities – in my own special place on this Earth.

When weather permits, I do much of my living outdoors. I have an outdoor patio where I can take my meals, a swinging bench from which I can greet passers-by while sipping a lazy afternoon beer, and a picnic table with benches by the brook. Being at the nexus of several popular hiking trails provides a steady stream of pedestrian traffic, so I never lack for company.

This house has an interesting history. During the 18th and 19th centuries, the rolling waters of Amethyst Brook were harnessed to power a number of small mills and factories. Among these were the Allen Sawmill and a fishing rod factory owned by Eugene P. Bartlett. In 1911, E.P. Bartlett purchased the sawmill property from Embert Harris in order to provide access from his factory to the town of Amherst. Harris was allowed to continue operation of the sawmill, leasing the land from Bartlett. Bartlett had a simple cabin and storage shed built for his use on the Amherst side of the property, presumably using lumber from the sawmill. A sign reading, "Mr. E.P. Bartlett," which was on

butcher-block counter that was once a bowling alley floor. The downstairs ceilings are 8' 4" high, while the upstairs ceilings are 5' 11" not counting slopes. The upstairs consists of two rooms, the smaller of which is my bedroom, with a futon on the floor by a window. To me, it feels like a loft in the treetops above the laughing brook. The other room I have partitioned into a library/computer area and a space

for guests. The guest area also serves me as an occasional retreat from the rest of the house. A skylight over the partition, along with two other sunny windows, ensures plenty of light and air. A small Monitor MPI 3800 heater at the bottom of the stairs keeps the entire house toasty warm in the winter, and between the shade of the trees and the cool waters of the brook, I have no need for air conditioning in the summer.

the shed when I purchased the property, now decorates my kitchen.

E.P. Bartlett died in 1925; unable to weather the Great Depression without his management, the fishing rod factory closed its doors, and its property was auctioned off. A small lot, including the cottage, shed, and some frontage on Amethyst Brook was purchased by Milo LaFogg.

Who was Milo LaFogg? The few references and recollections I have come across suggest a man who chose to live his own life his own way but was likeable and not without friends. He treasured his place of solitude by the brook, and threw himself wholeheartedly into transforming the simple cabin into a proper house with plumbing and electricity. He also put the house on a proper foundation, digging the 8' basement by hand. From what little I know, I have come to see much of myself in Milo, and much of Milo in myself. This is why I feel as if I were returning to a home I had built for myself in a previous life.

Since that time this cottage has been home to storytellers, puppeteers, young lovers starting their families and others, each adding their own imprint of creativity. Now it has come down (or back) to me.

Yes. I am a homeowner, perhaps one of the very few who purchased real estate in 2006 and did not come to regret it. But I think it would be closer to the truth to say that this house owns me. Even as I have chosen this house to be my home, I feel that in some sense I have been chosen by this house, and by the woodland spirits that live here, to be its caretaker. This house belongs here. I belong here.

Perhaps that is the best we can wish for, as we strive to find or create the home of our dreams – to find ourselves in a place where we belong.

Christopher Stoney is a self-confessed "old hippy" who has found a measure of prosperity and success working for an engineering firm but still clings to the old-fashioned values of peace, love and living in harmony in nature.

backyard studio – nicholas hunt

Almost surprising place for a tiny studio is this backyard in downtown Brooklyn where architect Nicholas Hunt designed and constructed his 55-sq.ft. backyard garden studio. He was able to build this 5' x 11' geometric design for under $1,200 by re-using materials salvaged from another job and taking white fence pickets from his parents' property for the interior. He used cedar cladding for the exterior, allowing it to weather with time. A small space like this needs a lot of light – so he designed wood-slatted windows and added a Plexiglas skylight. He shuts out the city by facing his windows toward nature. Construction took him seven days over a period of four months. It makes a perfect place to escape and relax – alone or with friends, and to use as a painting studio.

Nicholas Hunt is a registered architect in the State of New York where he works on a range of institutional and residential projects. He earned his Master of Architecture from Yale University and Bachelor of Architecture from Syracuse University.

Hunt-architecture.com

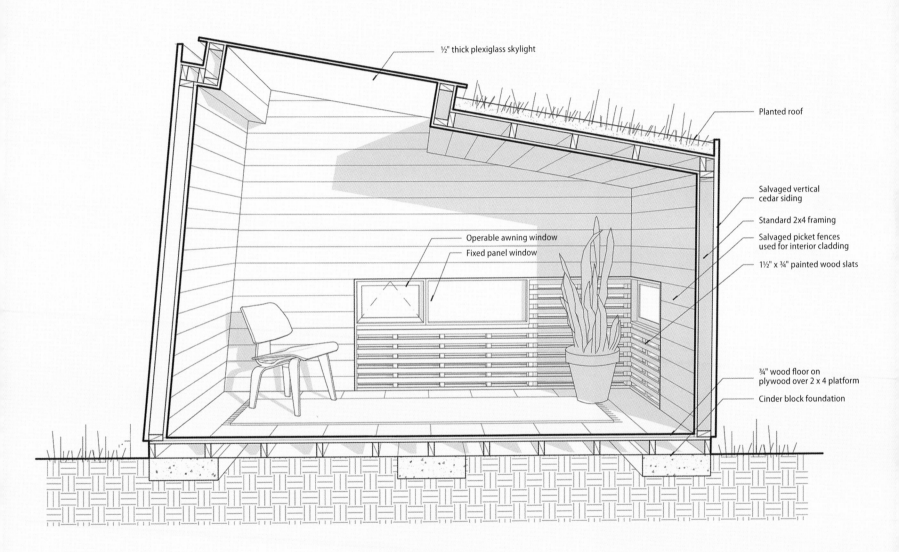

½" thick plexiglass skylight

Planted roof

Salvaged vertical
cedar siding

Standard 2x4 framing

Salvaged picket fences
used for interior cladding

1½" x ¾" painted wood slats

Operable awning window

Fixed panel window

¾" wood floor on
plywood over 2 x 4 platform

Cinder block foundation

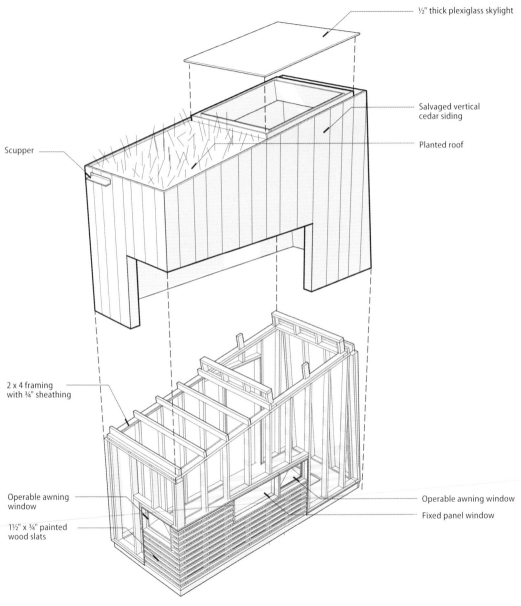

½" thick plexiglass skylight

Salvaged vertical cedar siding

Planted roof

Scupper

2 x 4 framing with ¾" sheathing

Operable awning window

Operable awning window

Fixed panel window

1½" x ¾" painted wood slats

Here are a couple other great tiny house concepts from Nicholas Hunt. Designed with kayakers and outdoor enthusiasts these building concepts are perfect for one-room recreation on the water. The one-room houseboat shown here features a raised sleeping platform, built-in storage and couches, a front and back deck, a roof garden and kayak storage.

The "Westport Kayak House" on page 190 is designed as a single room retreat and a place of relaxation and repose – a lovely kayak ride destination.

granny flat – michael trusty

As life expectancy increases, there are ever more senior citizens who need the comfort and security of family nearby. A "granny flat" can be the answer. Michael Trusty built this small adobe house for his mother, Jean, just a stone's throw away from his family home at the foot of the Sangre de Cristo Mountains. The design – a common effort between Jean, Michael and his wife, Jane – evolved during family discussions. Jean had firm ideas about certain aspects of the design. She did not want the new house to encroach on the family's privacy. She wanted a big porch (subsequently enclosed as a sun room). She wanted good views from the windows, a big bedroom with skylight and a library/guestroom. They chose a small minimalist kitchen, and used some of the saved space for a more luxurious bathroom. Light floods every room – entering from skylights and windows; the great views and sunsets always give the impression of being in a much larger house. The porch is glassed-in for year-round use and a feeling of being at one with nature.

Even though the house is small, there is more than enough room for children and grandchildren to stay over by making use of sofa-beds in both the living room and the coveted glassed-in porch with its panoramic view. The traditional adobe fireplace (or 'kiva') stands on a raised hearth, conveniently for a senior who is no longer quite so agile. The house allows Jean to maintain her independence in safety – a perfect granny flat.

Michael Trusty is a designer/builder and real-estate consultant in Santa Fe, New Mexico. His wife, Jane, is a real-estate appraiser; her expertise was also invaluable in putting the design ideas on paper.

ten and turning tiny- derek "deek" diedricksen

An early start in Cabins, Shelters, Tree Houses and Tiny Houses

I always had a fascination with structures so simple and vernacular that even as a kid I knew I could afford, and tackle, the dream of constructing one. And I more or less owe that early impetus to one man – well, outside of my very encouraging and very DIY-minded parents, and my ultra-scrimping "Mr. Fixit" of a grandfather. It was when I was gifted Lester Walker's book "Tiny Houses" the very year it came out (1986) that I realized that even on my scant lawn-mowing income, and with a dash of snow-shoveling coin, I could very well save up and build one of these, and own it, all by myself. I wasn't facing a "someday" dream, but saw the "here and now" of building small, and all without having to physically or financially kill myself to get there. I was a kid, nine years old – almost ten – and was already plotting, planning and mentally drooling over the prospect of owning my very own space where I, and not my parents, would be master of my own domain. Perhaps tiny housers are spatial control freaks, come to think of it? Whatever the case, mere months later, I was off, saving scraps of lumber from construction sites, hoarding and unbending the nails I could find, and saving what money I could muster for the unavoidable future purchasing of "adult" build materials like plywood and insulation. I was on a mission. I'd also make several fistfuls of mistakes, and that would

serve as one of the more thorough educations one could receive – "learn by doing." There is no better way. Books will only teach you so much. Sometimes the best course of action is to just jump in and get your feet wet. Sort things out as they hurtle your way.

The cabin I eventually was to build was an amalgamation of materials, one of differing levels of detail based on patience (or my available time away from pre-common-core math homework), and I'm sure would make for an interesting case-study of "making things up as you go along." The impetus to build, aside from being dazzled and inspired by the gorgeous array of classic cabins that Walker offered up in his book, was not so profoundly based in terms of its "need." I lived in a small two-bedroom, one-TV household, and yearned to have my own space. Let me clarify that: My own space to hide out and play video games until my bloodshot eyes couldn't take it anymore. Nintendo's first home gaming system had just come out, and I was taken with it – hook, line and sinker. Not so noble a reason for what I call my first "real," and "non-fort" build – but hey, its a start. Cut me some slack, I was ten years old. So the desire was planted, the inspiration was there, and I was off! I had already erected many tree houses, junk cabins, pallet forts and lean-tos. Now it was time to apply what I had learned on my own, in combination with some "big boy" techniques.

I did have a little help from my father, Glenn, when it came to a few of the trickier aspects of the cabin (crafting a homemade door and hanging it, for one). But I was able to complete this backyard cabin in around six months or so. My comic-book money was rerouted and depleted, my walk-to-town candy cash usurped and instead funneled into my new endeavor. My hands became blistered from lawn-mowing jobs *and* the build itself. But I was now in possession of a Cheshire Cat-like grin. I had done it. "The Cabin," as it had simply been dubbed, was now my den of Nintendo ("NinDENdo"?), my hideaway to write short stories on a vintage Smith Corona typewriter, and my haven from "The Fall Guy" re-runs in the main house. (I take that back: I loved that TV show.) The cabin was complete though, and at a not-so-grand and bizarrely sized 7' by 8' (due to some scrap lumber availability and to work-in room for an overhang in front using stock length eight footers) I now was the owner of a micro back-yard escape – one that possessed a built-in platform bed, was insulated and "wired" for electricity by means of a long extension cord from the main house. From this umbilical of power, I was able to power a small oil radiator for heat, and a black and white, 13" yard-sale TV (UHF dial and all). It was a basic build, but I was on my way. I had learned an unbelievable amount from getting up off my butt and "just doing it," and had learned even more from my blunders. On the non-budget of a ten-year-old kid, every bent nail, every miscut board and every flubbed framing arrangement was a wallet-pained move I wouldn't soon forget. And yes, I'd do it all over this way in a heartbeat.

So here I now am, an older, recovered video-game addict. I've built more tiny houses, cabins, backyard forts, backwoods shelters, funky greenhouses and unusual hobby spaces than I can remember. I'm addicted and passionate about what I do and

just love small spaces for so many reasons. Many of these reasons are most likely also shared by others – in fact I know they are, as I've talked to quite few tiny-house folks. The builders, dreamers, the designers and the dwellers all have their reasons, but here is a small list of the common ones – which I expand on a little more in my own book "Microshelters." I've since thought of a few new, or unlisted reasons too, which I've added here.

Why You Just Might Want to Rethink That BIG Project...

Small spaces require you to keep your life, tastes and spending habits to a minimum. Money burning a hole in your pocket? Desperate to get that new methane-powered vegetable slicer that transforms into a waffle maker too? Too bad. You don't have room for it. Discussion over; and you've just saved yourself from something you might not have needed, and from spending your hard-earned money. That impulse-buy crud located close to the checkout aisles? Same thing – no room.

Small structures are less site-invasive. You do not have to play "Georgia Pacific" and mow down acres of trees to build, and give access to your build spot. Tiny houses are often smaller than your average single car garage, and won't earn you the nickname "tree hater" when it comes time to build. Heck, some of the structures out there are so diminutive that you could *put* them up in a set of trees! Stranger things have been done. My original Vermont cabin at our "Tiny House Summer Camp" compound is a good example of this – we only had to cut down a single 8" diameter spruce to make room for the build.

A smaller dwelling is a heck of a lot more affordable (and quicker in this A.D.D. generation) to build! Want to save your money for the 70 years of student loan payments you still have (or for that golden zoot suit you've been eyeing)? Well, by living smaller, less of your money is going towards living. You now have more disposable income to do things (even foolish ones) with.

Environmentally you're often at an advantage with a smaller home. By costing less to heat, cool, furnish and maintain, you're pumping out less by way of pollutants into the air, using less in fossil fuels and being pretty frugal with your paint and touch-up materials over the years. And again, all of those things in reduced amounts, mean less time and money expended. You can work less, or earn less, to pay for these scaled-back basics. *That* sounds pretty darn sensible, and awesome, to me.

"Less to clean" is a pretty huge reason as to why many want to "go tiny." If your mindset is "I'd much rather French kiss a viper than vacuum my home," then a tiny, or smaller house, might be for you! Some houses are so small that their owners don't even own vacuum cleaners – they just sweep them, or periodically pull their 6' x 8' rug out to beat it with a broom. And dusting your house? If it's small enough, a good sneeze might be all that's required.

Small space edifices are more likely to be projects you can undertake without the aid of a whole armada of helpers. This is key, as, let's face it, there are only so many times you can bribe your friends with BBQ to come

out and help you, and the other alternative of hiring professionals can end up a bank-breaker. Schedules of most people in this over-worked day and age are rather sporadic, to say the least. The possibility of building and actually completing your smaller space project is greater, as you can employ the "hunt and peck" method: Work on the build with snatches of time here and there when they present themselves. You can also build as funds allow. It's usually a "no race" situation for most.

You get the idea. As for my personal look at, and reasons for loving, "tiny," for me it's a creative, affordable and fun way to create manageable, cozy and whimsical spaces. Whether it be kids' forts, full-out tiny houses, or treehouses, I think one part of my attraction to these spaces is rooted in my upbringing as a kid. Why would I want those times and memories to end? I can continue my youthful pursuits and additionally create new memories, and new fun directions in micro architecture. I can continue to explore the problem-solving paths of trying to build with recycled and salvaged materials. Why shouldn't I?

But wait, there's more!

I'm going to leave you with one of *the best* building and designing tips that you'll ever be candidly handed. I see workshop hosts and YouTube videos gloss over this all the time as if the creators are perfect. Let me assure you – they aren't. So here it is: You *will* mess up – quite possibly a lot. It's just part of the battle. The key is to know this ahead of time, brace yourself for it, and not let it conquer you. When the inevitable happens, you've hopefully saved yourself from what otherwise could be a mental meltdown. "Embrace The Mistakes," I always tell my students. When (not *if* but *when*) you make a mistake, sometimes the lesson learned is invaluable. Better yet, sometimes the creative paths you have to invent to climb out of the error will make for a better, more daring and unique design or approach in the end product. This may sound asinine to you right now, but I'm hoping some of you will discover this as you build. Possibly you'll even enjoy these detours and thrive because of them.

Derek "Deek" Diedricksen is the author of the bestselling books "Microshelters" and "Humble Homes, Simple Shacks, Cozy Cottages, Ramshackle Retreats, Funky Forts" as well as the building zine "Quick Camps and Leg Cramps." Derek and his brother Dustin have hosted hands-on tiny house- and shelter-building classes "From Fargo to Sydney," and run the YouTube channel "relaxshacksDOTcom" – a companion to the blog www.relaxshacks.com. Deek and Dustin were hosts/designers for the HGTV series, "Tiny House Builders" and have had their work featured in The New YorkTimes, the homepage of yahoo.com, The Boston Globe, on many TV shows, at SxSW, in magazines, and beyond.

Deek's favorite tiny house/cabin design EVER? The Bolt Together House by Jeff Milstein.

glossary

batten- a thin narrow strip of wood used to seal, reinforce or support a joint

bird's mouth joint- a V-shaped joint that is often used to connect a rafter to a wall's top plate

blind nailing- a nailing technique used for fastening tongue and groove boards; nails are set at an angle

cant strip- a strip placed in the angle between a roof and the joining wall

cats- horizontal timbers in a structure (used in between studs, connecting them)
cleats- a narrow board or strip used as a support

dado- a three-sided trench cut across the grain of a board

fascia- a horizontal piece covering the joint between the top of a wall and the overhanging eaves

ferro-cement- mortar or plaster applied over mesh and some sort of reinforcements (such as rebar)

gables- the angled wall that meets the end of a pitched roof

groove- a three-sided trench cut with the grain of a board

lap joint- an overlapping joint in which one piece of wood, the thicker of the two, has its thickness reduced to accept the full thickness of the other board

mortise- a recess cut into a piece to receive a tenon

muntin- a thin strip that separates panes of glass in a sash

pork chop- a triangular piece of scrap lumber

R-value- a measurement of an insulating material's effectiveness; the higher the R-value, the more insulating a material is
rabbet- a two-sided trench cut on the edge of a board

rip-cut- a cut parallel to the grain of the board

shiplap- a wooden board with rabbets on opposites sides allowing the boards to overlap

soffit- the underside of a structure such as overhanging eaves

spline- a narrow strip of wood that is glued in corresponding grooves to join pieces of wood

stile- the vertical member of any frame, such as a door, window or face frame

stringers- a timber used to support cross members (in stairs, the stringer supports the treads)

studs- vertical timbers in a structure

tenon- the rabbeted edge that is inserted into a matching recess, called a mortise

timber-frame construction- a centuries-old building technique for joining heavy timbers with mortise and tenon joints secured by oak pegs called trunnels

toenail- the act of driving a nail at an angle through a board to attach it to another

tongue and groove- a method of joining boards, such as flooring, by inserting a thin ridge on one edge (tongue) into a thin slot on the other (groove)

treads- the cross members on stairs or ladders

trunnel- a wooden peg used to fasten timbers together

resources

Insulation
www.homedepot.com
- denim insulation
- rockwool insulation

Lighting
www.sunforceproducts.com
Solar hanging light with remote.

www.bensdiscountsupply.com
Humphrey Gas Light: Model # 9HPB

Stoves & Heaters
www.lehmans.com; 800-438-5346
- Small camp stove - model #25410

www.northerntool.com
- Vogelzang Stoves - Boxwood cast iron stove - model #BX26E
- Cast iron woodburning stove - model #2421

www.hwam.com (contemporary wood-burning stoves)

Mr. Heater Portable Buddy Propane Heater – 9000 BTU,
- model# MH9BX - for spaces up to 200 sq. ft.

www.campchef.com - Ranger Series Blind Stoves (2 or 3 burners)

www.mrheater.com (solar or propane heaters)

Water:
www.bosch.com - tankless on-demand water heater, 80 gallon, model #RP17PT

www.campchef.com - Triton hot water heater - portable gas-powered water heater. Also available at www.walmart.com

www.coleman.com
- 5-gallon collapsible water carrier
- Powermax Grill Stove (grill & burner)

www.myivation.com - solar powered portable shower

www.sunfrost.com - solar refrigeration

www.potableaqua.com - Potable Aqua, Purification tablets – water purification tablets

www.humanurehandbook.com
- Loveable Loo eco-toilet
- The Humanure Handbook by Joseph Jenkins – all about eco-toilets

Mini-Kitchens:
www.avantiproducts.com
Ready-made mini-kitchens

Miscellaneous
www.andersenwindows.com - doors (# NLGD8068) & windows (Japanese Guest House)

www.yestertec.com - Yestertec Design Company (kitchens)

www.homedepot.com - willow fencing for roof, 3'3" high x 13' (Japanese Guest House)

www.bestmaterials.com - EPDM – Flat rubber roofing membrane (Japanese Guest House)

www.lowes.com
- Tuftex carbonate corrugated roofing
- ReliaBilt 300 Series - glass sliding "patio" doors, #71980-1223722
- Vanity cabinets, faucets, marble counters

www.homedepot.com
Mirrored wall cabinets with built-in lights

www.menards.com
MDO plywood

www.McFeelys.com
Screws, tools & more including:
#10 washer-head screws

www.recycledproductsco.com
Barn window sashes (Tudor Backyard Cottage)

Books/Reading Sources:

"Backyard Building" by Jeanie & David Stiles

"Cabins – A Guide to Building Your Own Nature Retreat" by David & Jeanie Stiles

"Sheds – The Do-It-Yourself Guide for Backyard Builders" by David & Jeanie Stiles Designs

"Workshops You Can Build" by David & Jeanie Stiles

"Rustic Retreats – A Build-It-Yourself Guide" by David & Jeanie Stiles

"Microshelters: 59 Creative Cabins, Tiny Houses, Tree Houses, and Other Small Structures" by Derek "Deek" Diedricksen

"Humble Homes, Simple Shacks, Cozy Cottages, Ramshackle Retreats, Funky Forts" by Derek "Deek" Diedricksen

"Tiny Tiny Houses" by Lester Walker (The first book about tiny houses.)

"Shedworking" by Alex Johnson (Describes how the U.K. has turned sheds into home offices.)

"Black & Decker Codes for Homeowners"

"Black & Decker Complete Guide to Wiring"

Helpful Websites:

www.relaxshacks.blogspot.com
Deek Diedricksen's site with lots of imaginative ideas for living smaller. His latest books is Micro-Shelters – filled with great stuff.

www.tinyhouseblog.com
Living Simply in Small Spaces
Kent Griswold discusses tiny house construction and living.

www.thetinylife.com
www.tinyhousechat.com
Ryan Mitchell is a leading Tiny House Movement source. The Tiny Life is a resource for those seeking information on tiny living, which encompasses simple living, tiny houses and environmentally responsible lifestyles. More than just information on tiny houses, this blog includes discussions on living life… tiny!

https://www.adventure-journal.com/2016/01/mail-order-cabins-make-a-comeback/
Muji's mail-order cabins.

www.heartofitallhouse.com
www.facebook.com/heartofitallhouse
Instagram@heartofitallhouse
Trevor Gay – great small house building source

www.tinyhousetalk.com
"The purpose of Tiny House Talk is to spread the message of freedom, peace and happiness through simple living."
From people who live in 120 sq. ft. tiny houses on wheels to those who live in 825 sq. ft. solar powered homes and just about anything else in between.

www.Nichedesignbuild.com
"Shrink your footprint. Expand your world."

www.theboatgalley.com
Great space-saving advice from Carolyn Shearlock who lives on a sailboat.

www.yestermorrow.org
Design and build workshops including how to design and build your own tiny house.

www.tumbleweedhouses.com
Portable tiny houses on wheels. Workshops and plans listed; blogs.

www.resourcesforlife.com/small-house-society
"Better Living Through Simplicity." Greg
Johnson.

www.tinyhousebuild.com
Andrew Morrison provides workshops, books
and teaches people how to build their own
homes.

www.tinyhouse.net
Tiny house insight and instructions from
Ethan Waldman, an experienced tiny house
builder, owner and dweller.

http://www.fastcoexist.com/3056129/this-house-costs-just-20000-but-its-nicer-than-yours/1
A site describing building a house for under
20K.

www.treehugger.com
A site about the pros and cons of building a
tiny house and "green" architecture.

index

credits

Distributed in the U.K. and Europe by
F+W Media International, LTD
Pynes Hill Court
Pynes Hill
Rydon Lane
Exeter
EX2 5SP
Tel: +44 1392 797680
Visit our website at popularwoodworking. com or our consumer website at shopwood-working.com for more woodworking information.

Other fine Popular Woodworking Books are available from your local bookstore or direct from the publisher.

ISBN-13: 978-1-4403-4546-3

21   20   19   18   5   4   3   2

READ THIS IMPORTANT SAFETY NOTICE

To prevent accidents, keep safety in mind while you work. Use the safety guards installed on power equipment. When working on power equipment, keep fingers away from saw blades, wear safety goggles to prevent injuries from flying wood chips and sawdust, wear hearing protection and consider installing a dust vacuum to reduce the amount of airborne sawdust in your woodshop. Don't wear loose clothing or jewelry when working on power equipment. Tie back long hair to prevent it from getting caught in your equipment. People who are sensitive to certain chemicals should check the chemical content of any product before using it. The authors and editors who compiled this book have tried to make the contents as accurate and correct as possible. Plans, illustrations, photographs and text have been carefully checked. All instructions, plans and projects should be carefully read, studied and understood before beginning construction. Due to the variability of local conditions, construction materials, skill levels, etc., neither the author nor Popular Woodworking Books assumes any responsibility for any accidents, injuries, damages or other losses incurred resulting from the material presented in this book. Prices listed for supplies and equipment were current at the time of publication and are subject to change.

Editor: *Scott Francis*
Copy Editor: *Toby Haynes*
Cover Designer: *Daniel Pessell*
Interior Designer: *Laura Spencer*
Illustrator: *David Stiles*
Production Coordinator: *Debbie Thomas*

METRIC CONVERSION CHART

Inches	Centimeters	2.54
Centimeters	Inches	0.4
Feet	Centimeters	30.5
Centimeters	Feet	0.03
Yards	Meters	0.9
Meters	Yards	1.1

a content + ecommerce company

Ideas ▪ Instruction ▪ Inspiration

Receive FREE downloadable bonus materials when you sign up for our FREE newsletter at **popularwoodworking.com**.

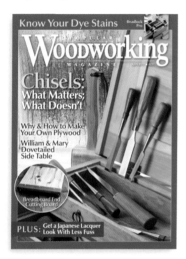

Visit **popularwoodworking.com** to subcribe (look for the red "Subscribe" button on the navigation bar).

These and other great Popular Woodworking products are available at your local bookstore, woodworking store or online supplier. Visit our website at **shopwoodworking.com**.

Visit our Website

Find helpful and inspiring articles, videos, blogs, projects and plans at **popularwoodworking.com**.

 For behind the scenes information, become a fan at **Facebook.com/ popularwoodworking**

 For more tips, clips and articles, follow us at **twitter.com/ pweditors**

 For visual inspiration, follow us at **pinterest.com/ popwoodworking**

 For free videos visit **youtube.com/ popularwoodworking**

 Follow us on Instagram **@popularwoodworking**

Popular Woodworking Videos

Subscribe and get immediate access to the web's best woodworking subscription site. You'll find more than 400 hours of woodworking video tutorials and full-length video workshops from world-class instructors on workshops, projects, SketchUp, tools, techniques and more!

videos.popularwoodworking.com